TWO NICHIREN TEXTS

BDK English Tripiṭaka 104-III, 104-V

TWO NICHIREN TEXTS

Risshōankokuron
(Taishō Volume 84, Number 2688)

Kanjinhonzonshō
(Taishō Volume 84, Number 2692)

Translated from the Japanese

by

MURANO Senchū

Numata Center
for Buddhist Translation and Research
2003

First Printing, 2003
ISBN: 1-886439-17-6
Library of Congress Catalog Card Number: 2003100192

Published by
Numata Center for Buddhist Translation and Research
2620 Warring Street
Berkeley, California 94704

Printed in the United States of America

A Message on the Publication of the English Tripiṭaka

The Buddhist canon is said to contain eighty-four thousand different teachings. I believe that this is because the Buddha's basic approach was to prescribe a different treatment for every spiritual ailment, much as a doctor prescribes a different medicine for every medical ailment. Thus his teachings were always appropriate for the particular suffering individual and for the time at which the teaching was given, and over the ages not one of his prescriptions has failed to relieve the suffering to which it was addressed.

Ever since the Buddha's Great Demise over twenty-five hundred years ago, his message of wisdom and compassion has spread throughout the world. Yet no one has ever attempted to translate the entire Buddhist canon into English throughout the history of Japan. It is my greatest wish to see this done and to make the translations available to the many English-speaking people who have never had the opportunity to learn about the Buddha's teachings.

Of course, it would be impossible to translate all of the Buddha's eighty-four thousand teachings in a few years. I have, therefore, had one hundred thirty-nine of the scriptural texts in the prodigious Taishō edition of the Chinese Buddhist canon selected for inclusion in the First Series of this translation project.

It is in the nature of this undertaking that the results are bound to be criticized. Nonetheless, I am convinced that unless someone takes it upon himself or herself to initiate this project, it will never be done. At the same time, I hope that an improved, revised edition will appear in the future.

It is most gratifying that, thanks to the efforts of more than a hundred Buddhist scholars from the East and the West, this monumental project has finally gotten off the ground. May the rays of the Wisdom of the Compassionate One reach each and every person in the world.

NUMATA Yehan
Founder of the English
Tripiṭaka Project

August 7, 1991

Editorial Foreword

In January 1982, Dr. NUMATA Yehan, the founder of the Bukkyō Dendō Kyōkai (Society for the Promotion of Buddhism), decided to begin the monumental task of translating the complete Taishō edition of the Chinese Tripiṭaka (Buddhist canon) into the English language. Under his leadership, a special preparatory committee was organized in April 1982. By July of the same year, the Translation Committee of the English Tripiṭaka was officially convened.

The initial Committee consisted of the following members: (late) HANAYAMA Shōyū (Chairperson), BANDŌ Shōjun, ISHIGAMI Zennō, KAMATA Shigeo, KANAOKA Shūyū, MAYEDA Sengaku, NARA Yasuaki, SAYEKI Shinkō, (late) SHIOIRI Ryōtatsu, TAMARU Noriyoshi, (late) TAMURA Kwansei, URYŪZU Ryūshin, and YUYAMA Akira. Assistant members of the Committee were as follows: KANAZAWA Atsushi, WATANABE Shōgo, Rolf Giebel of New Zealand, and Rudy Smet of Belgium.

After holding planning meetings on a monthly basis, the Committee selected one hundred thirty-nine texts for the First Series of translations, an estimated one hundred printed volumes in all. The texts selected are not necessarily limited to those originally written in India but also include works written or composed in China and Japan. While the publication of the First Series proceeds, the texts for the Second Series will be selected from among the remaining works; this process will continue until all the texts, in Japanese as well as in Chinese, have been published.

Frankly speaking, it will take perhaps one hundred years or more to accomplish the English translation of the complete Chinese and Japanese texts, for they consist of thousands of works. Nevertheless, as Dr. NUMATA wished, it is the sincere hope of the Committee that this project will continue unto completion, even after all its present members have passed away.

It must be mentioned here that the final object of this project is not academic fulfillment but the transmission of the teaching of the

Buddha to the whole world in order to create harmony and peace among humankind. To that end, the translators have been asked to minimize the use of explanatory notes of the kind that are indispensable in academic texts, so that the attention of general readers will not be unduly distracted from the primary text. Also, a glossary of selected terms is appended to aid in understanding the text.

To my great regret, however, Dr. NUMATA passed away on May 5, 1994, at the age of ninety-seven, entrusting his son, Mr. NUMATA Toshihide, with the continuation and completion of the Translation Project. The Committee also lost its able and devoted Chairperson, Professor HANAYAMA Shōyū, on June 16, 1995, at the age of sixty-three. After these severe blows, the Committee elected me, Vice President of Musashino Women's College, to be the Chair in October 1995. The Committee has renewed its determination to carry out the noble intention of Dr. NUMATA, under the leadership of Mr. NUMATA Toshihide.

The present members of the Committee are MAYEDA Sengaku (Chairperson), BANDŌ Shōjun, ISHIGAMI Zennō, ICHISHIMA Shōshin, KANAOKA Shūyū, NARA Yasuaki, TAMARU Noriyoshi, URYŪZU Ryūshin, YUYAMA Akira, Kenneth K. Tanaka, WATANABE Shōgo, and assistant member YONEZAWA Yoshiyasu.

The Numata Center for Buddhist Translation and Research was established in November 1984, in Berkeley, California, U.S.A., to assist in the publication of the BDK English Tripiṭaka First Series. In December 1991, the Publication Committee was organized at the Numata Center, with Professor Philip Yampolsky as the Chairperson. To our sorrow, Professor Yampolsky passed away in July 1996. In February 1997, Dr. Kenneth K. Inada became Chair and served in that capacity until August 1999. The current Chair, Dr. Francis H. Cook, has been continuing the work since October 1999. All of the remaining texts will be published under the supervision of this Committee, in close cooperation with the Editorial Committee in Tokyo.

MAYEDA Sengaku
Chairperson
Editorial Committee of
the BDK English Tripiṭaka

Publisher's Foreword

The Publication Committee shares with the Editorial Committee the responsibility of realizing the vision of Dr. Yehan Numata, founder of Bukkyō Dendō Kyōkai, the Society for the Promotion of Buddhism. This vision is no less than to make the Buddha's teaching better known throughout the world, through the translation and publication in English of the entire collection of Buddhist texts compiled in the *Taishō Shinshū Daizōkyō,* published in Tokyo in the early part of the twentieth century. This huge task is expected to be carried out by several generations of translators and may take as long as a hundred years to complete. Ultimately, the entire canon will be available to anyone who can read English and who wishes to learn more about the teaching of the Buddha.

The present generation of staff members of the Publication Committee includes Marianne Dresser; Brian Nagata, president of the Numata Center for Buddhist Translation and Research, Berkeley, California; Eisho Nasu; and Reverend Kiyoshi Yamashita. The Publication Committee is headquartered at the Numata Center and, working in close cooperation with the Editorial Committee, is responsible for the usual tasks associated with preparing translations for publication.

In October 1999, I became the third chairperson of the Publication Committee, on the retirement of its very capable former chair, Dr. Kenneth K. Inada. The Committee is devoted to the advancement of the Buddha's teaching through the publication of excellent translations of the thousands of texts that make up the Buddhist canon.

Francis H. Cook
Chairperson
Publication Committee

Contents

RISSHŌANKOKURON

Contents

Translator's Introduction

The *Risshōankokuron* was written as an appeal to the Japanese government in 1260 by Nichiren (1222—1282). On the sixteenth day of the seventh month of that year, Nichiren's text was delivered to ex-regent Hōjō Tokiyori by his personal secretary Yadoya-saemon-no-jō. At that time, the ex-regent still held the reins of power in the government.

The official head of the Kamakura government, established in 1192, was the shogun, a military dictator. In 1205, however, the real power of the government was held by the regent. For seven years, from 1256 to 1263, the power of the regency was in the hands of ex-regent Hōjō Tokiyori. For all practical purposes, the Kamakura government–in the person of the ex-regent–ruled Japan at the time Nichiren wrote this work.

Nichiren was a native of the province of Awa, in the southern part of present-day Chiba Prefecture. He became a monk in a Tendai temple of that province in 1233. At that time the tenets of the Tendai school were much influenced by Shingon mysticism and Nembutsu devotionalism. Thus Nichiren was familiar with these various schools of Buddhist thought from his early days. From 1242 to 1253 he studied at Mount Hiei and elsewhere.

Nichiren was a faithful adherent of the teachings of T'ien-t'ai Chih-i Ta-shih (Tendai Chisha Daishi), founder of the T'ien-t'ai (Tendai) school. His intention was to restore the pure form of T'ien-t'ai Buddhism, which was based on the teaching expounded in the *Saddharmapuṇḍarīka-sūtra* (*Lotus Sutra;* also referred to in this text by its Japanese title, *Hokekyō*). To Nichiren, the *Lotus Sutra* was the source of the true teaching of the Buddha. Any opinion or interpretation of Buddhist doctrine that ran counter to the *Lotus*

Sutra was, to his mind, an enemy of Buddhism. It was unbearable to him that the *Lotus Sutra* was ignored by Hōnen, founder of the Nembutsu school.

While the Nembutsu school, which emphasized the practice of worshiping Amitābha Buddha, had been established long before his time, Hōnen was the first Nembutsu priest to disregard the *Lotus Sutra* in his writings and teaching. Equally galling to Nichiren was the fact that Nembutsu devotionalism was extremely popular, attracting many commoners as well as members of the samurai class. The practice of worshiping Amitābha was not foreign to older schools, which recognized the Nembutsu as a secondary teaching. In order to cope with the rise of Hōnen's Nembutsu school, these older schools encouraged the practice of worshiping Amitābha as outlined in their own school's tenets. The result was that the great majority of Japanese people were followers of this practice, while devotion to Śākyamuni Buddha was relegated to a scant few of the older temples. It was Nichiren's most fervent desire to restore Śākyamuni Buddha to the forefront of popular Japanese practice.

In this text, Nichiren is concerned more with social realities than with metaphysics. The *Risshōankokuron* takes the form of a dialogue between a traveler and a master about the troubled state of affairs in the country, which has been beset by "disasters, famine, and pestilence." In his own time Nichiren witnessed many such calamities, including earthquakes, famine, outbreaks of plague, and civil war.

Worse, Nichiren believed that Japan was facing an impending foreign invasion from the Asian continent. The Mongol chief Temuchin (1162—1227) had established a kingdom in present-day Mongolia in 1206, calling himself Jenghiz Khan. In quick succession, his army invaded Chin, a country in Northern China, in 1211, and occupied the capital of Yenching in 1215. Jenghiz Khan's progeny continued to dominate Asia. In 1234 his eldest son Ogotai took Chin. His grandson Mangu occupied Southern China, including the region of present-day Vietnam, in 1251. Mangu's brother Kublai Khan subjugated Korea in 1258. The word "Mongol" is not directly mentioned in the *Risshōankokuron,* but judging from the imaginative descriptions of a possible invasion of Japan by foreign armies in this work, Nichiren must have had ample information of the activities of the Mongols in China and Korea.

The threat of foreign invasion prophesied in this work may have irritated government officials. What was likely even more annoying to them, however, was Nichiren's reference to the former emperor Gotoba. Hōjō Shigetoki, father-in-law of ex-regent Hōjō Tokiyori, had been one of the officials who ordered Gotoba exiled to the island of Oki in 1221.

Nichiren' s criticism of the Hōjō regency may have begun from the first day of his ministerial activities. The *Risshōankokuron* can be viewed as a collective expression of Nichiren's thought and opinions up to 1260. While the Buddhist temples of Kamakura flourished under the auspices of the Hōjō family, what awaited Nichiren after his presentation of the *Risshōankokuron* was not patronage but persecution. He was exiled to Itō a year later; Hōjō Shigetoki was an active player in the government's decision to banish Nichiren from Kamakura.

A Note on the Translation

Except for the *Lotus Sutra,* which is referred to in both Sanskrit (*Saddharmapuṇḍarīka-sūtra*) and romanized Japanese (*Hokekyō*), the names of Buddhist texts quoted in this work appear in romanized Japanese, with the Sanskrit (where applicable) and/or romanized Chinese title given on first appearance, along with the title in English. The names of Chinese figures and dynasties are given in romanized Chinese, followed by their romanized Japanese equivalent on first appearance.

RISSHŌANKOKURON

OR

THE TREATISE ON THE ESTABLISHMENT OF THE ORTHODOX TEACHING AND THE PEACE OF THE NATION

by

Nichiren, Śrāmaṇa of Japan

Dialogue I

The Cause of the Calamities

The traveler says sorrowfully:

"In recent years there has been much disaster, famine, and pestilence all over the country. Cows and horses lie dead on the roadsides and skeletons are scattered on the streets. Most of the population [of this country] is already dead. I cannot help lamenting all this. 203a5

"[In order to avert these calamities] some call the name of the Teacher of the Western World (Amitābha Buddha), believing [the statement of Shan-tao (Zendō) that calling the name of the Teacher of the Western World] is the sharpest sword [to cut off evil karma]. Some recite the sutra dedicated to the Buddha of the East (Bhaiṣajyaguru) who vowed that he will cure the diseases [of those who hear his name]. Some treasure the excellent statement in the *Saddharmapuṇḍarīka-sūtra (Lotus Sutra; Hokekyō)*, [in which] the true teaching [of Śākyamuni Buddha is expounded, that a sick person who hears this sutra] will be cured of his disease and not grow older or die. Some hold the ceremony of giving a hundred lectures [on the *Ninnōkyō* (*Kāruṇikārājāprajñāpāramitā-sūtra; Sutra of a Benevolent King*) according to the statement in the sutra that] seven calamities [in a country] will turn into seven felicities [if the king of that country lectures on this sutra]. Some sprinkle water from five vases over offerings in accordance with esoteric Shingon rites. Some practice *zazen* and concentrate their minds in order to see the truth of emptiness as clearly as they see the bright moon. Some write the names of the seven gods and post them on gates. Some make images of the five [bodhisattvas] of great power and hang them on doors. Some practice exorcism at the four corners [of a city] and pray to the gods of heaven and earth.

"Government authorities take various benevolent measures out of compassion for the people. But their painstaking efforts are to no avail. The people have become even more hungry and pestilence more rampant. Beggars and the dead are seen everywhere [on the streets]. Piles of corpses resemble platforms and lined-up bodies look like bridges.

"The sun and the moon shine bright and the five planets make a chain of brilliant gems. The Three Treasures are honored in this country; and the line of a hundred emperors [of this country] has not yet come to the end. But why has this country deteriorated so soon? Why has the Dharma perished? What kind of evil or mistake is reponsible for this situation?"

The master says:

"I have long been lamenting over these calamities. Now I know that you have also. Let us talk!

"It is to attain Buddhahood through the teaching [of the Buddha] that one renounces his family and becomes a monk. Now I see that no Shintō or Buddhist gods can do anything [to avert these calamities]. Judging from this, I cannot believe that I shall be able to be reborn [in a Buddha land and attain Buddhahood] in a future life [by practicing the teaching of the Buddha]. This may be a result of my ignorance. I cried with regret, looking up to the sky, and thought [about the cause of the calamities], lying with my face on the ground.

"I racked my poor brains and read sutras [to find out the cause of the calamities. At last I have reached the following conclusion]. The people of this country are standing against the Right Dharma. They believe wrong teachings. Thus, the gods have deserted this country. Saints have left us and they will never return. *Māra*s and devils have come instead and calamities have taken place. I cannot help saying this. I cannot help but to dread this."

Dialogue II

Predictions in the Sutras

The traveler says:

"Not only I but all the people of this country lament over these calamities. Now I have come here and heard from you that these calamities have taken place because the gods and saints have left us. What sutras say so? I want to hear the references [to the cause of such calamities in the sutras], if any." 203b

The master answers:

"There is much evidence in the sutras. In the *Konkōmyōkyō* (*Suvarṇaprabhāsa-sūtra; Sutra of Golden Light*) [the four great heavenly kings tell the Buddha]:

> [Suppose that] although this sutra exists in a country it is not propagated there yet. The king of that country ignores this sutra and does not wish to hear it, make offerings to it, or respect or praise it. He does not respect or make offerings to the four kinds of devotees (monks, nuns, laymen, and laywomen) who uphold this sutra when he sees them. As a result, we, our attendants, and the other innumerable gods will not be able to hear the profound and wonderful Dharma [expounded in this sutra], nor drink nectar or obtain the Right Dharma. Consequently, we will lose our light and power. Living beings in the evil realms will increase, and those in heavenly and human realms will decrease. Living beings will fall into the river of birth and death (samsara), and depart from the Way to nirvana. World-honored One! If we four [great heavenly] kings and our attendants including *yakṣa*s see all this, we will leave that country and give up the intention to protect it. Not only we but also the innumerable great gods

> who are supposed to protect that country will leave that king. After we and those gods depart, that country will suffer from various calamities. The king will be dethroned. The people will not have any good thoughts. There will be arrests, murders, quarrels, slander, and flattery. Innocent people will be punished. Pestilence will prevail. Comets will appear from time to time. Two suns will rise at the same time. The darkenings and eclipses of the sun and moon will become irregular. A black rainbow will appear together with a white one and make an ill omen. There will be shooting stars. The earth will quake. Voices will be heard from the bottoms of wells. Rainstorms and windstorms will come unseasonably. Famines will take place one after another. Seedlings will not grow. Plants will not bear fruit. The armies of many other countries will invade the country, and the people will undergo many kinds of suffering. They will lose the places where they might live peacefully.

"The *Daijikkyō* (*Mahāsaṃnipāta-sūtra; Great Collection Sutra*) says:

> When the Dharma disappears, [monks] will have long beards, hair, and nails, and my precepts will be forgotten. Loud voices will be heard from the sky, and the earth will quake. All things will shake just as on a waterwheel. The walls of cities will crumble and houses will collapse. The roots, branches, leaves, flowers, fruits, and flavors of the fruits of trees will disappear. The living beings of the whole realm of desire (*kāmadhātu*) [and the realm of form (*rūpadhātu*)], except those of the Heaven of Pure Abode, will be deprived of food of the seven tastes. Those living beings will also lose the three kinds of energy. All the excellent commentaries on the teaching of liberation will also disappear. Flowers and fruits will be without fragrance and flavor. All the wells, springs, and pools will dry up. Land will be brackish and sterile. Fields will be split into hills and ravines.

> Mountains will erupt. Dragons in heaven will not send rain. Seedlings will die.... Plants will die. Even weeds will not grow. Dust will rain down and obscure the light of the sun 203c
> and moon. Everything will be dried up all over the land, and many ill omens will be seen from time to time. [The king and monks of that country] will commit the ten evil acts, and their greed, anger, and ignorance (i.e., the three poisons) will increase. The people will ignore their parents just like deer do. They will decrease in number. Their lives will be shortened. Their physical power will be weakened, and their pleasures will diminish. They will be deprived of the pleasures of gods and humans and sent to the evil realms [in their future lives]. When the evil king and monks eliminate my Right Dharma by committing the [ten] evil acts and decrease the worlds of heavenly and human beings, all the gods who are compassionate toward all living beings will abandon that defiled country and go to other places.

The *Ninnōkyō* says:

> When a country is thrown into disorder, devils will first become active in that country. When they become active, the people [of that country] will be in chaos. That country will be invaded by its enemies, and many people will be killed. The king, crown prince, other princes, and government officials will quarrel with each other. Disorder will be seen in heaven and on earth. The movements of the twenty-eight constellations, the sun, and the moon will become irregular, and many rebellions will break out.

"The Buddha says in the same sutra:

> Seeing [the world] throughout the three periods (past, present, and future) clearly with my five kinds of eyes, I have arrived at the conclusion that all kings have been able to obtain their thrones because they attended five hundred Buddhas in their previous existences. Therefore, all saints

> [including] arhats will appear in their countries and give great benefits to the kings. When the merit of the kings expires, the saints will leave their countries. Seven calamities will take place [there] after the departure of the saints.

"The *Yakushikyō* (*Bhaiṣajyaguruvaiḍūryaprabhāsapūrvapraṇidhānaviśeṣavistara; Sutra of Bhaiṣajyaguru*) says:

> The calamities that will trouble the duly inaugurated king and other *kṣatriyas* [of a country] are pestilence, foreign invasions, rebellions, disorder in the movements of the constellations, darkenings and eclipses of the sun and the moon, unseasonable windstorms and rainstorms, and famine.

"The Buddha addresses [King Prasenajit] in the *Ninnōkyō*:

> Great king! My teachings extend over ten billion Mount Sumerus and as many suns and moons. Each Mount Sumeru is surrounded by four continents. In the southern continent called Jambudvīpa there exist sixteen great countries, five hundred medium-sized countries, and ten thousand small countries. Each country will suffer from seven calamities. [If] a king [reads this sutra] in order to [avert] these calamities, [the seven calamities will turn into seven felicities].
>
> What are the [seven] calamities?
>
> The sun and the moon do not move regularly; the seasons do not follow one another regularly; a red or black sun rises; two, three, four, or five suns rise at the same time; the sun is eclipsed and its light is lost; or the sun is surrounded by one, two, three, four, or five haloes.... All this is the first calamity.
>
> The movements of the twenty-eight constellations become irregular; and the gold star, comets, ring star, devil star, fire star, water star, wind star, funnel star, south ladle stars, north ladle stars, largest planet, king star, three minister stars, and a hundred official stars change their appearances from time to time.... All this is the second calamity.

> The living beings as well as the non-living beings of a country are burned by great fires; or fires are caused by devils, dragons, gods, mountain spirits, humans, trees, or bandits.... All this is the third calamity.
>
> Great floods drown people; the seasons do not follow 204a
> one another regularly; it rains in winter and snows in summer; thunder rolls and lightning flashes in winter; it freezes, frosts, and hails in the sixth month; red, black, or blue rains fall; earth mountains or rock mountains fall from the sky; sand, gravel, or stones fall from the sky; rivers flow upstream, cause mountains to float, or wash away stones.... All this is the fourth calamity.
>
> Great winds blow people away to their deaths; mountains, rivers, and trees are blown away at the same time; untimely gales or black, red, or blue winds or the winds of heaven, of the earth, of fire, or of water blow.... All this is the fifth calamity.
>
> Everything is dried up; the ground is dry deep down; much grass dies; the five kinds of cereals do not ripen; land looks as if it were burned; and many people die.... All this is the sixth calamity.
>
> The country is invaded by the armies of surrounding countries; rebellions break out; bandits take advantage of fires, floods, gales, or devils to torment people; and wars break out. All this is the seventh calamity.

"The *Daijikkyō* says:

> Suppose there is a king who practiced almsgiving, kept the precepts, and cultivated wisdom in innumerable previous existences. If he sees that my Dharma is perishing and does not protect it, the innumerable roots of goodness that he planted [in his previous existences] will perish. His country will suffer from three misfortunes: 1) a rise in the price of grain [because of famine], 2) war, and 3) pestilence. The gods will leave his country. The people will not obey his

> orders. His country will always be invaded by its enemies. Fires will break out everywhere; many windstorms will blow people away; many rainstorms will drown them; and the relatives of the king will revolt against him. The king will soon become seriously ill and he will be sent to a great hell after his death.... So too will the queen, crown prince, ministers, headmen of cities and villages, generals, county governors, and prime ministers.

"The meaning of the above quotations from the four sutras is clear and indubitable. The blind and distracted [leaders of this country] believe the wrong teachings and do not understand the Right Dharma. [Misled by them,] the people have deserted all the Buddhas [except those honored by the leaders] and ignore the sutras [other than those chosen by those leaders]. They do not wish to support [other] Buddhas and sutras. [They have eliminated the Three Treasures in the true sense of the word by despising the right teaching of the Buddha.] Therefore, the gods and saints have abandoned this country, and devils and heretics have created calamities."

Dialogue III

Priests of Today

The traveler says with anger:

"Emperor Ming-ti (Meitei) of the Later Han (Kan) dynasty met a golden man in his dream and obtained sutras [brought by priests mounted] on white horses. Crown Prince Jōgū suppressed the anti-Buddhist movement of [Mononobe-no-]Moriya and founded a Buddhist temple. Since then, all the emperors and people [of this country] have been worshiping Buddhist images and reciting Buddhist sutras. Buddhist images and sutras are honored in Enryakuji, the temples of Nara, Onjōji, Tōji, and in as many other temples with as many sutras as there are stars and clouds in the 204b
sky, built all over this country including the five provinces around Kyoto and the provinces lying along the seven national highways. Some priests as wise as Śāriputra are making efforts to obtain wisdom as bright as the moon hanging above [Mount] Gṛdhrakūṭa while others as well disciplined as Haklena are practicing meditation [just as Mahākāśyapa did] on Mount Kukkuṭapāda.

"You say that the [blind and distracted leaders] have eliminated the Three Treasures [in the true sense of the word] by despising the [right] teaching of the Buddha. Who are they? Tell me about them in detail!"

The master admonishes:

"There are row upon row of temples and sutra storehouses. Priests as numerous as rice plants, hemp plants, bamboo trees, or reeds receive respect day after day, year after year. But they are not good. They flatter [almsgivers] and mislead people. Government officials are too ignorant to know right from wrong.

"The *Ninnōkyō* says:

> Suppose bad monks seek fame and gain in a country. A teaching that will destroy both the country and the Buddha-Dharma will be expounded by them to the king, crown prince, and other princes. The king who believes their teaching thoughtlessly will promulgate laws inconsistent with the precepts of the Buddha, and destroy both the country and the Buddha-Dharma

"In the *Nehangyō* (*Nirvana Sutra*) the Buddha addresses [the bodhisattvas]:

> Bodhisattvas! Do not be afraid of evil elephants! Be afraid of evil friends!... When you are killed by an evil elephant, you will not be sent to the three evil realms. But when you are killed by an evil friend, you will go there.

"In the *Saddharmapuṇḍarīka-sūtra* [the eighty billion *nayuta* bodhisattvas address the Buddha]:

> Some monks in the evil world will be cunning. They will flatter [almsgivers]. Thinking that they have obtained what they have not yet obtained, their minds will be filled with arrogance. They will live in remote places and wear patched pieces of cloth. Believing that they are practicing the True Way, they will despise others. Being attached to worldly profits, they will expound the Dharma to men in white robes. They will be given the same respect by the people of the world as the arhats who have attained the six supernatural powers.... In order to speak ill of us in the midst of the great multitude, in order to slander us, in order to say that we are bad, they will say to kings, ministers, brahmans, householders, and monks that we have wrong views and that we are expounding the teaching of heretics.... There will be many dreadful things in the evil world of the *kalpa* of defilements. Devils will enter the bodies [of those monks]

> and cause them to abuse and insult us. . . . Bad monks in the defiled world will speak ill of us, grimace at us, or drive us out of our monasteries from time to time without knowing that what you have expounded hitherto is [not the true teaching but only] expedient teachings given according to the capacities of living beings.

"In the *Nehangyō* the Buddha says:

> After my nirvana, my right teaching will be preserved for numberless centuries (the Age of the Right Teaching of the Buddha). [In that period there will live] four kinds of saints. After that period the counterfeit of my right teaching will be propagated (the Age of the Counterfeit of the Right Teaching of the Buddha). There will be no saints. The monks in the latter period (the Age of Degeneration) will keep my precepts in form only. They will only partially read and recite sutras. They will be indulgent in eating and drinking and live an easy life.... Although they may wear the robes of monks, they will [flatter almsgivers] as carefully as a hunter stalks his game or as a cat watches a rat. They will claim that they have already attained arhatship.... They are greedy and jealous but will pretend to be wise and good. They will resemble the brahmans who praise silence. Although they are not *śrāmaṇa*s, they will pretend to be so. They will strongly advocate wrong views and slander the Right Dharma.

"The priests of today are like the monks described in these 204c
sutras. How can we hope to accomplish anything without criticizing them?"

Dialogue IV

The One-sided Teaching

Furious, the traveler protests:

"A wise king leads his people according to universal principles. A sage governs his country on the basis of knowledge of right and wrong. The people of this country take refuge in and trust the priests of today. A wise king does not believe in evil priests. The priests of today are saintly because they are respected by wise men. Why is it that you speak ill of them? Why do you call them evil priests? Tell me about them in detail!"

The master replies:

"[I will tell you about them later. Here I must speak about Hōnen.] Hōnen wrote the *Senchakushū* (*Senchaku Hongan Nembutsu Shū; A Collection of Passages on the Nembutsu Chosen in the Original Vow*) during the reign of the regnant ex-emperor Gotoba. He misinterpreted the teaching of the Buddha and misled all the people of this country [by this writing]. His *Senchakushū* says:

> Tao-ch'o (Dōshaku) says that there are two kinds of teaching of the Buddha, the teaching for saints and the teaching of the Pure Land, and that we should give up the teaching for saints and take refuge in the teaching of the Pure Land....
>
> There are two kinds of teachings for saints: [the Hinayana and the Mahayana. There are two sets of divisions of the Mahayana: esoteric Mahayana and exoteric Mahayana on one hand, and True Mahayana and Provisional Mahayana on the other. Tao-ch'o excludes the esoteric Mahayana and the True Mahayana from the teaching for saints.] I

think that the esoteric Mahayana and the True Mahayana also should be included [in the teaching for saints].... Therefore all of the eight schools, the Shingon, Busshin, Tendai, Kegon, Sanron, Hossō, Jiron, and Shōron schools, should be included [in the teaching for saints]....

T'an-luan (Donran) says in his *Ōjōronchū* (*Wang sheng lun chu; Commentary on Vasubandhu's Discourse on the Pure Land*), "According to Nāgārjuna's *Daśabhūmika-vibhāṣā-śāstra* (*Exposition of the Ten Stages*), there are two ways, the difficult way or the easy way, for a bodhisattva to attain the stage of non-retrogression. The difficult way is the teaching for saints and the easy way is the teaching of the Pure Land.... Those who are studying the Jōdo (Pure Land) school should know this. If a person who has been studying the teaching for saints wishes to be born in the Pure Land, he should give up the teaching for saints and take refuge in the teaching of the Pure Land."

Shan-tao says that there are two kinds of practices, right practices and miscellaneous practices, and that we should give up miscellaneous practices and perform right practices.... [There are five miscellaneous practices.] The first is to keep, read, and recite the Hinayana sutras, and the esoteric and exoteric Mahayana sutras, excluding the *Kammuryōjukyō* (*Amitāyurdhyāna-sūtra; Sutra on Contemplation of Amitāyus*) and other sutras that talk about rebirth in the Pure Land.... The third miscellaneous practice is to worship Buddhas, bodhisattvas, and gods other than Amitābha Buddha.

[It says in the *Ōjōraisan* (*Wang sheng li tsan; Hymns of Birth in the Pure Land*) that a hundred out of a hundred persons who perform the right practices exclusively will be reborn in the Pure Land of Amitābha Buddha, but that even one out of a thousand persons who perform the miscellaneous practices will not be reborn there.]

From this I can say that we should give up the miscellaneous practices and perform right practices exclusively. How can we give up the exclusive performance of right practices leading a hundred out of a hundred persons to the Pure Land? How can we cling to the miscellaneous practices that do not lead even one out of a thousand persons to the Pure Land? Practitioners should think well on this.

"The *Senchakushū* also says:

A list of Mahayana sutras, including those of the esoteric and exoteric Mahayana, is given in the *Jōgennyūzōroku* (*Chen-yüan ju ts'ang lu; Chen-yüan Catalogue of Scriptures Collected in the Piṭakas*). The list begins with the *Mahāprajñāpāramitā-sūtra* (*Great Perfection of Wisdom Sutra*) compiled in six hundred volumes and ends with the *Hōjōjūkyō* (*Fa ch'ang chu ching; Sutra on the Omnipresence of the Dharma*). These Mahayana sutras are six hundred thirty-seven in number, compiled in two thousand eight hundred eighty-three volumes. The practice of reading and reciting the Mahayana sutras should be regarded as one [of the good deeds that can be practiced with a distracted mind].... Know this: When the Buddha expounds according to the capacities of his hearers, he opens the gate to two kinds of good deeds: good deeds that can be practiced with a distracted mind, and good deeds that cannot be practiced without a concentrated mind. But when he expounds the Dharma of his own accord [without taking the capacities of his hearers into consideration], he shuts the gate to these two kinds of good deeds. The gate that once opened will never be shut is the gate of calling the name of Amitābha Buddha. 205a

"The *Senchakushū* also says:

Those who call the name of Amitābha Buddha should have the three states of mind. The *Kammuryōjukyō* says....

The commentary on this sutra says:

> *Question:* What will you say when you are asked by men of wrong views who study and practice differently from you [whether calling the name of Amitābha Buddha will lead you to his Pure Land]?
>
> [*Answer:* I will tell them the following parable] in order to correct their wrong views. [Suppose a man travels to the west. He comes to a river a hundred feet wide. The river is divided into two parts by a white path four or five inches wide. Fire is on the south of the white path; and water is on the north side of the white path. The white path is constantly washed by waves and burned by flames. A voice is heard from the east, telling him to proceed. A man on the west bank of the river tells him to come. Bandits live on the east bank of the river. They want to catch the traveler. When the traveler proceeds a step or two along the white path, the bandits tell him to come back. He does not listen to them. He proceeds singleheartedly, and reaches his destination. In this parable the teaching of Śākyamuni Buddha is likened to the voice heard from the east.] Men of wrong views who study and practice differently...are likened to the bandits who tell the traveler to come back when he proceeds a step or two [along the white path. Amitābha Buddha is likened to the man on the west bank of the river.]
>
> Men of wrong views who study and practice differently are those who practice the teaching for saints.

"The *Senchakushū* says in conclusion:

> Those who wish to quickly leave the world of birth and death should abandon the teaching for saints and take refuge in

the teaching of the Pure Land. Those who wish to take refuge in the teaching for the Pure Land should abandon the miscellaneous practices and perform right practices.

"It was Tao-ch'o's mistake to say that there are two kinds of teaching of the Buddha: the teaching for saints and the teaching of the Pure Land. It was T'an-luan's mistake to say that there are two ways: the difficult way and the easy way. It was Shan-tao's mistake [to say that there are two kinds of practice: right practices and miscellaneous practices. Hōnen] followed them and categorized upholding the six hundred thirty-seven Mahayana sutras in two thousand eight hundred eighty-three volumes expounded by Śākyamuni Buddha, including the *Saddharmapuṇḍarīka-sūtra* and the sutras of the Shingon school, and [worshiping] the Buddhas, bodhisattvas, and gods [except Amitābha Buddha] as miscellaneous practices, as the teaching for saints, and as the difficult way. [Hōnen said that] we should give up [the teaching for saints], shut [the gate to the sutras], desert [the teaching for saints], and abandon [the miscellaneous practices]. Thus he misled people. Worse still, he slandered all the saintly priests of the three countries, that is, the disciples of Śākyamuni Buddha of all the countries, by comparing them to bandits.

"According to the canonical sutras of the Jōdo school, [Amitābha Buddha] vowed [during his bodhisattvahood], '[When I attain Buddhahood, I will cause those who call my name to be reborn in my world] except those who have committed the five grave offenses or slandered the Right Dharma.' [Hōnen] was against this vow.

"The *Hokekyō* is the most important of all the sutras expounded during the five periods of teaching. [Hōnen] ignored [Śākyamuni's] warning in the second volume of this sutra, 'Those who do not believe this sutra and slander it...will fall into the Avīci Hell when they die.'

"This is the Age of Degeneration. There are no saints. All people are led into a blind alley. They have forgotten the direct way [to Buddhahood]. Alas! No one awakens them. What a pity! Wrong teachings have become more and more popular. Therefore not only the emperor but also the commoners [of this country] think that there are no sutras other than the three sutras of the Jōdo school, and that there is no Buddha other than Amitābha who is accompanied by the two bodhisattvas [Avalokiteśvara and Mahāsthāmaprāpta].

"Dengyō, Gishin, Jikaku, and Chishō crossed the sea of ten thousand waves and traveled over the mountains and through the valleys of China. They brought back Buddhist images and sutras [to this country], and founded temples on mountains and
205b in valleys to enshrine them. Śākyamuni Buddha and Bhaiṣajyaguru Buddha emitted light, illuminating the people during and after this life. Ākāśagarbha Bodhisattva and Kṣitigarbha Bodhisattva taught and benefited them also, during and after this life. Therefore emperors and local lords donated land to the temples and made offerings [to the Buddhas and bodhisattvas].

"But since Hōnen's *Senchakushū* was published, our Original Teacher (Śākyamuni) has been forgotten, and the Buddha of the Western Land has been honored instead. The Buddha of the East, whom [Dengyō] taught us to worship, has been deserted. Only the four volumes of the three sutras [of the Jōdo school] are read and recited, and all the other sutras expounded through the five periods of the teaching [of Śākyamuni] have been abandoned. No one makes offerings to temples other than those enshrining Amitābha Buddha, or to priests other than those who call the name of Amitābha Buddha. Therefore temples [except those enshrining Amitābha Buddha] are dilapidated. Grass grows on the roofs and weeds cover the gardens. No one wishes to support or rebuild those temples. Therefore no saintly priests live there; no guardian gods stay there. This was caused purely by the publication of Hōnen's *Senchakushū*. Alas! For the past several decades, many people have been led astray, deceived by the devil. They have forgotten the Right Dharma, and preferred an insignificant teaching. How can the gods refrain from anger? Many people have given up a perfect teaching and preferred a one-sided teaching.

Will devils miss the chance to take advantage of their mistake? Rather than perform ten thousand prayers, we should eliminate [this one-sided teaching]."

Dialogue V

Ill Omens

The traveler says very angrily:

"The three sutras of the Jōdo school were expounded by Śākyamuni Buddha, our Original Teacher. T'an-luan gave up the teachings expounded in the four *śāstra*s and took refuge exclusively in the Pure Land teaching. Tao-ch'o first studied various practices expounded in the *Nehangyō,* but later propagated the practice for [rebirth in] the Western Land exclusively. Shan-tao gave up the miscellaneous practices and called the name of Amitābha Buddha exclusively. Eshin Sōzu collected quotations from sutras and considered calling the name of Amitābha Buddha to be the most important practice. Amitābha Buddha has been honored in this way for a long time. I do not know how many people so far have been reborn in his world [by calling his name].

"Hōnen Shōnin entered the temple on the mountain of the Tendai school while young, completed his study of [the commentaries on the *Saddharmapuṇḍarīka-sūtra* in] sixty volumes and the tenets of the eight schools at the age of seventeen. He read all the sutras and *śāstra*s seven times. He also perused all the other Buddhist philosophical and biographical works. His wisdom was as bright as the sun and moon. His virtues excelled those of all his predecessors. With all this, however, he could not find the way out [of birth and death] to nirvana. Therefore, he thought over the way, at last abandoning all the sutras [except those of the Jōdo school], and devoted himself to the practice of calling the name of Amitābha Buddha. According to the inspiration given him in his dream, he propagated this practice to all the people of the country. [For the past several decades] since then, he has been respected as the reincarnation of Mahāsthāmaprāpta Bodhisattva or Shan-tao. He is honored by all the people of this country, noble or humble, male or female.

205c You show disrespect to the sutras [of the Jōdo school] expounded by Śākyamuni Buddha, and criticize the comments on Amitābha Buddha. You ascribe the recent calamities to a teaching expounded in the past, and blame not only the predecessors [of the Jōdo school] but also [Hōnen] Shōnin. You blow the hair of others to find out their ugly points. You cut the skin of others to let blood flow. I have never heard such blasphemy. You should be ashamed of yourself. You should be careful about what you say. You have committed a grave sin. You will have to be punished. I cannot bear talking with you. I want to take up my cane and leave.

The Master smiles and the traveler pauses. The Master then says:

"You will be accustomed to taking spicy food if you constantly eat smartweed leaves. You will forget the bad smell if you stay in a lavatory for a long time. Good words are taken for bad ones. Slanderers of the Right Dharma are called saints; and teachers of the Right Dharma, bad priests. Your mistakes are serious. Your sins are not minor. Listen! I will explain [the cause of the calamities] in more detail.

"The Buddha expounded provisional teachings before the true teaching, [which he expounded in the fifth] of the five periods of his teaching. T'an-luan, Tao-ch'o, and Shan-tao honored his earlier teachings and ignored his last teaching. They did not understand the true teaching of the Buddha. Neither did Hōnen who had followed them. Hōnen misled people by using the words 'give up,' 'shut,' 'desert,' and 'abandon' in connection with the six hundred thirty-seven Mahayana sutras compiled in two thousand eight hundred eighty-three volumes, and with the Buddhas, bodhisattvas, and gods. All that he says is his personal opinion, not based on any sutra. That [opinion] is not true. That [opinion] is a blasphemy. You cannot reproach him too much.

"The people of today believe him and honor his *Senchakushū*. Thus, the three Pure Land sutras are respected but all the other sutras are abandoned. The Buddha of the happiest world (i.e., Amitābha) is honored but all the other Buddhas are forgotten. Hōnen is an enemy of all the Buddhas and sutras and of all people, including saintly priests. Now his teaching is propagated all over this country. You are furious at me for saying that the recent calamities have been caused by a teaching expounded in the past. To prove my point, I will cite some historical precedents:

"A quotation from the *Shiki* (*Shih-chih; Record of History*) is given in the *Makashikan* (*Mo he chih kuan; Great Calming and Insight*), Volume II. It says, 'Toward the end of the Chou (Shū) dynasty, there lived an ill-mannered man whose hair was disheveled and whose shoulders were bare.' The *Shikanguketsu* (*Chih kuan hung chüeh*), Volume II, comments on this passage as follows:

> It says in the *Saden* (*Tso-ch'uan*) that when King P'ing-wang (Hei-ō) of the Chou dynasty moved the capital of his country [to Lo-i (Raku-yu)] in the east, a man with disheveled hair was holding a ceremony in the field at I-ch'uan (Isen)[, near the capital].
>
> [Seeing the ill-mannered man officiating at the ceremony,] a wise man said, "[I-ch'uan] will be occupied [by a foreign army] within a hundred years because manners have already been lost there." [This prophecy turned out true.] From this we see that an ill omen appears before a calamity takes place.

"[The *Makashikan*, Volume II,] says:

> [The *Shiki* says:] ["At the beginning of the Ch'in (Shin) dynasty] there lived a man called Yüan-chi (Genseki). He was clever but indifferent to his appearance. He had disheveled hair and a loose sash. His ill manners became popular among the members of the nobility of that country. Blaming each other with vulgar words was taken for living

a natural life, and observance of manners was regarded as the behavior of unrefined people.

"This [disregard for manners] proved to be an ill omen of the downfall of the Ssu-ma (Shiba) family, [who had founded the Ch'in dynasty]."

"Jikaku Daishi [discusses the worship of Amitābha Buddha in China] in his *Nittōjunreiki* (*Ennin's Diary*). His discussion may be summarized as follows:

> By order of Emperor Wu-tsung (Buso) of the T'ang (Tō) dynasty, Dharma Master Ching-shuang (Kyōso) of Chang-ching-ssu (Shākyōji) visited many temples in the first year of Hui-ch'ang (Kaishō). He lectured on the practice of calling the name of Amitābha Buddha for three days at each temple. The army of the Uighurs invaded T'ang in the second year of Hui-ch'ang. The governor of the district north of the Yellow River revolted against the emperor in the third year of Hui-ch'ang. Soon after that, Tibet refused imperial
> 206a orders; and the army of the Uighurs invaded T'ang again. Rebellions and foreign invasions ensued, and houses in cities and villages were burned just as in the period from the end of the Ch'in dynasty to the beginning of the Han dynasty. Emperor Wu-tsung suppressed Buddhism by destroying many temples, but could not suppress the rebellions or defend his country against foreign invaders. [He died in agony in the sixth year of Hui-ch'ang.]

"Hōnen was active in the years of Kennin under the reign of the regnant ex-emperor Gotoba. Since this was a recent event, all of us know that the ex-emperor [died in exile]. Here we see the historical consequences [of the propagation of the practice of calling the name of Amitābha Buddha] in the great T'ang and in our country. You cannot doubt [these facts]. You should give up the evil practice and take refuge in the Right Dharma. You should stop the fountainhead. You should cut out the root."

Dialogue VI

Appeals to the Emperor and Shogun

The traveler calms down. He says:

"I think I understand you a little bit. [What I do not understand is the following.] If you are right, an appeal for the ban of that practice must have already been submitted to the emperor or to the shogun, because there are many Buddhist leaders in Kyoto and Kamakura. As it is, none of them has submitted an appeal. You are but a low-ranking priest. Besides, your talk is too spiteful [to persuade others]. You are achieving nothing."

The Master says:

"I have been fortunate enough to study the Mahayana although I am an incompetent person. A fly can travel ten thousand miles when it clings to the tail of a horse. Ivy plants can stretch themselves for a thousand yards when they creep on the trunk of a pine tree. As a son and disciple of the Buddha, I am now attending the King of Sutras (*Lotus Sutra*). How can I refrain from lamenting over the decline of the Buddha's teaching?

"The *Nehangyō* says:

> Know this! A monk is an enemy of the Buddha's teaching if he does not reproach, persecute, or punish a destroyer of the Buddha's teaching. [A monk] who does this is my disciple, a true *śrāvaka*.

"Although I am not a good monk, I do not want to be called an enemy of the teaching of the Buddha. Therefore, I have outlined some [historical facts]. Moreover, appeals [for the ban of the ill-omened practice] were submitted to the emperor and the shogun by Enryakuji and Kōfukuji during the Gennin period. By orders of the emperor and shogun, both of whom wished to repay the favors given them by the Buddhas of the past, present, and future, the printing blocks of the *Senchakushū* were sent to the Daikōdō and burned there; the tomb of Hōnen was destroyed by the servants of the Kanjin-in; and Ryūkan, Shōkō, Jōkaku, and Sasshō, all of whom were disciples of Hōnen, were banished to remote places. They have not yet been pardoned. You are wrong in saying that no one has submitted an appeal [for the ban of that practice]."

Dialogue VII

The Warnings of the Buddha

The traveler recovers his equanimity and says:

"I have too little knowledge to criticize a sutra or a priest. I clearly understand that [Hōnen] used the words 'give up,' 'shut,' 206b 'desert,' and 'abandon' in connection with the six hundred and thirty-seven Mahayana sutras compiled in two thousand eight hundred and eighty-three volumes, and in connection with the Buddhas, bodhisattvas, and gods. But are you aware that you blame him only for his use of these words? I do not know whether you are wise or not. I cannot decide whether you are right or not. You contend all the more vehemently that the recent calamities are caused by the publication of the *Senchakushū*.

"The peace of our country is wished for not only by the government but also by all the people. A country prospers when it abides by the Dharma [expounded by the Buddha]. The Dharma is respected by the people of a country [that abides by it]. When a country is destroyed and the people of that country are annihilated, no one will honor the Buddha or believe the Dharma. We should first pray for the peace of our country and then establish the Buddha-Dharma. [In order to realize the peace of our country, we must stop the calamities.] How shall we stop them? Tell me the means [to do so], if any."

The Master says:

"I am too ignorant to have my own opinion [about the means to avert calamities]. Therefore, I cannot do anything but try to find the means in the sutras. There are many references to the means of stopping calamities not only in Buddhist sutras but also in non-Buddhist writings. Those references are too many to quote here. As far as Buddhist sutras are concerned, it can be concluded that the peace of our country will be realized if slanderers of the Right Dharma are eliminated and keepers of the Right Dharma are respected.

"The *Nehangyō* says:

> The Buddha tells [Cunda], "Almsgiving to anyone is praiseworthy, except to a particular kind of person."
>
> Cunda asks [the Buddha], "What kind of person is excepted?"
>
> The Buddha says, "A violator of the precepts who is discussed in this sutra is excepted."
>
> Cunda says again, "I do not yet understand your explanation. Please explain it again!"
>
> The Buddha tells Cunda, "One who violates the precepts is called an *icchantika*. Those who give alms to anyone, except to an *icchantika*, will be praised and will receive great rewards."
>
> Cunda asks [the Buddha] again, "Explain the meaning of '*icchantika*' in more detail."
>
> The Buddha says, "Cunda! An *icchantika* is a monk (*bhikṣu*) or nun (*bhikṣuṇī*), or a male or female lay devotee (*upāsaka* or *upāsikā*), who slanders the Right Dharma with evil words and does not repent of this evil karma; or who commits the four grave deeds, the five grave offenses, and does not repent of or confess his or her offenses although he or she is aware of being guilty; or who does not wish to protect or to establish the Right Dharma but slanders or despises it with evil words.... Those who give alms to anyone except an *icchantika* will be praised by others."

"The Buddha says to [Maitreya Bodhisattva] in the same sutra:

> I remember that I became the king of a great country in Jambudvīpa in a previous existence. At that time my name was Foreseer. I loved and respected the sutras of the Great Vehicle. I was pure and good in mind. I had no evil thought.

> I was not jealous of others. I did not begrudge anything.... Good man! I protected the Great Vehicle. At that time 206c
> I heard some brahmans slandering the Great Vehicle. Having heard this, I killed them. Good man! Because of this, I have never fallen into hell since then.

"The same sutra also says:

> [Kāśyapa Bodhisattva asks the Buddha,] "You killed the brahmans when you were performing bodhisattva practices as a king in a previous existence. [Why did you kill them?]"
>
> The Buddha answers, "I killed them because I wished them to stop slandering the Great Vehicle and to practice the Good Dharma in their future lives."

"The Buddha tells [Kāśyapa Bodhisattva] in the same sutra:

> There are three kinds of killing: minor, medium, and major. Minor killing is to kill ants or other animals. Those who commit minor killing will fall into hell or to the realms of animals or hungry ghosts. They will endure minor suffering because animals have a small amount of roots of goodness. But to kill animals into which bodhisattvas have transformed themselves [in order to save others] cannot be regarded as minor killing. Medium killing is to kill human beings who are in stages from the stage of a stream-winner (*srota-āpanna*), a once-returner (*sakṛdāgāmin*), or a non-returner (*anāgāmin*). Those who commit medium killing will fall into hell or to the realms of animals or hungry ghosts. They will endure medium suffering. Major killing is to kill one's parents, arhats, *pratyekabuddha*s, or bodhisattvas who have reached the stage of non-retrogression. Those who commit major killing will fall into the great Avīci Hell.... Good man! To kill *icchantika*s is not regarded as any of the three kinds of killing. Good man! Those brahmans [whom I killed in my previous existence] were *icchantika*s.

"The Buddha tells King Prasenajit in the *Ninnōkyō:*

> Therefore, I will transmit [this sutra] to kings, not to monks or nuns [or to male or female lay devotees] because [the four kinds of devotees] are not as powerful as kings.

"The Buddha says in the *Nehangyō:*

> Now I will transmit the unsurpassed Right Dharma to kings, ministers, prime ministers, and the four kinds of devotees.... They should eliminate those who slander the Right Dharma.

"The Buddha tells [Kāśyapa Bodhisattva] in the same sutra:

> Kāśyapa! My body is as indestructible as a diamond. I was able to receive it because I protected the Right Dharma [in a previous existence]....Good man! Those who [wish to] protect the Right Dharma need not keep the five precepts or live a monastic life. They should carry swords, bows, arrows, and halberds with them....The keepers of the five precepts are not men of the Great Vehicle. Those who protect the Right Dharma are men of the Great Vehicle even though they do not keep the five precepts. Those who [wish to] protect the Right Dharma should carry swords and other weapons with them.... Those who carry swords and sticks with them [for the purpose of protecting the Right Dharma] shall be called keepers of the precepts....
>
> Good man! There lived a Buddha called Joy Increasing in this city of Kuśinagara.... After his nirvana, his right teaching was preserved for a period of many hundreds of millions of years. During the last forty years of that period, there appeared a monk called Enlightenment Virtue. He kept the precepts.... Many monks who had violated the precepts heard him expounding the Dharma. They had evil intentions. They attacked this teacher with swords and
> 207a sticks. The king of that country was called Having Virtue. Having Virtue heard that the monk was in danger. The king

immediately came to him and fought those evil monks in order to protect the Dharma. The expounder of the Dharma was saved. The king had cuts and wounds from swords and halberds all over his body. Not even a part of his skin the size of a poppy seed was left unhurt. Enlightenment Virtue praised the king, saying, "Excellent, excellent! You protected the Right Dharma. You will be able to receive the innumerable teachings [of the Buddha and become a Buddha] in the future."

Having listened to the Dharma, the king was delighted. Immediately after, he died and was reborn in the Buddha land of Akṣobhya. He became the first disciple of that Buddha. All his generals, soldiers, subjects, and attendants, who had joined the fighting and had been delighted [to listen to the Dharma] sought *bodhi* without retrogression. After their deaths, they were also reborn in the land of Akṣobhya Buddha. Enlightenment Virtue was also reborn in the land of Akṣobhya Buddha after his death, and became the second disciple of that Buddha.

If you see the Right Dharma being destroyed, you should keep and protect it as they did. Kāśyapa! The king was I. The monk who expounded the Dharma was Kāśyapa Buddha. Kāśyapa! Anyone who protects the Right Dharma will be given such immeasurable rewards as are stated above. Because I protected the Right Dharma in a previous existence, I am now able to possess this eternal, indestructible body which is adorned with various excellent physical marks....

Therefore, the laymen who wish to protect the Dharma should carry swords and sticks with them [as the king and his men did].... Good man! After my nirvana, the world will be defiled and will deteriorate. All the countries of the world will be thrown into disorder. They will invade each other, and many people will starve. Many people will become monks only for the purpose of getting food. They will be false monks.

When they see a monk who protects the Right Dharma, they will drive him away or kill or hurt him.... Therefore, a monk who keeps the precepts is allowed to be accompanied by laymen who carry swords and sticks with them.... Those laymen also shall be called keepers of the precepts. Although they carry swords and sticks with them, however, they should not kill [the false monks even when those false monks kill a monk who protects the Right Dharma].

"The *Saddharmapuṇḍarīka-sūtra* says:

Those who do not believe this sutra but slander it destroy the seeds of Buddhahood in all living beings of the world.... They will fall into the Avīci Hell when their present life ends.

"The above quotations from the sutras are quite clear. They need no comment. According to the *Saddharmapuṇḍarīka-sūtra,* the slanderers of the Mahayana sutras are worse than those who commit the five grave offenses endlessly. They will fall into the great Avīci Hell and never get out of it. According to the *Nehangyō,* you can give alms to those who commit the five [grave] offenses, but cannot give alms to slanderers of the Right Dharma. Those
207b who kill ants will fall into one of the three evil realms, but those who kill slanderers of the Right Dharma will certainly reach the stage of non-retrogression. Kāśyapa Buddha was Enlightenment Virtue. Śākyamuni was Having Virtue. The *Saddharmapuṇḍarīka-sūtra* and the *Nehangyō* are the most important of all the sutras that the Buddha expounded during the five periods of his teaching. The Buddha's warnings in these sutras are imperative. Who would not take them up?

"But the slanderers of the Right Dharma ignore the keepers of the Right Dharma. They treasure Hōnen's *Senchakushū* and become blind and ignorant. They adore Hōnen and make images of him. They believe his deluded teachings, print his dangerous words, cherish them, and propagate them all over the country.

Many people have converted to his faith. They make offerings only to his disciples. They change the hand signs (*mudrās*) of the images of Śākyamuni Buddha into those of the images of Amitābha Buddha. They replace the images of the Buddha of the East with those of the Teacher of the Western World. The *Hokekyō* has been used as a text for hand-copying for more than four hundred years. But now the sutra is replaced by the three Pure Land sutras. The memorial service for T'ien-t'ai [Chih-i] Ta-shih has been changed into the service for Shan-tao.

"The people [who have converted to the faith of Hōnen] are too many to count. Are they not destroying the Buddha, Dharma, and Sangha (the Three Treasures)? Their wrong views come from the *Senchakushū*. Alas! They do not heed the sincere warnings of the Buddha. What a pity! They follow the misleading words of ignorant priests. If you wish to realize the peace of our country quickly, you should eliminate these slanderers of the Right Dharma from our country."

Dialogue VIII

How to Establish the Right Dharma

The traveler says:

"You say that those priests ignore the warnings of the Buddha and slander the Right Dharma and that we should eliminate them [from our country]. Do you mean to say that we should kill them as is suggested [in the *Nehangyō*]? If so, we will have to commit killing endlessly. Our retribution will be terrible."

"The *Daijikkyō* says:

> All gods and humans should make offerings to anyone who has his head shaven and wears the robe of a monk, whether he keeps the precepts or not.... To make offerings to him is to make offerings to me.... He is my son.... To strike him is to strike my son. To speak ill of him is to speak ill of me.

"From this I can say that we should make offerings to any priest, whether he is good or not, whether he is right or not. How can we strike a son and make his father sad? [A brahman called] Bamboo Stick was in the Hell of Incessant Suffering for a long time after he killed the Venerable Maudgalyāyana. Devadatta was choked with the smoke of the flames of the Avīci Hell for a long time after he killed a nun called Lotus Flower. The descriptions of the retribution for killing monks and nuns are clearly given [in the sutras]. You appear to be correct in criticizing the slanderers of the Dharma, but are you not actually contradicting the precepts of the Buddha? I cannot believe what you say. What do you think of this?"

The master says:

"You have seen the quotations from the sutras, and still say this. Do you not understand them? Is their meaning not clear to

207c you? I am not saying that we should not make offerings to priests [who commit minor offenses] but that we should not do so to priests who slander the Right Dharma. The Buddha says that we should stop making offerings to those [who slander the Right Dharma]. He does not tell us to kill them, although he killed them in his previous existence. If the four kinds of devotees of all the countries of the world stop making offerings to evil priests and take refuge in the Good Dharma, no calamity will take place."

Dialogue IX

How to Save Our Country

Showing respect by moving back and resettling himself, the traveler says,

"There are various teachings of the Buddha. They are difficult to understand, with many points that are beyond my comprehension. It is not clear to me which teaching is right. But what Hōnen Shōnin meant to say in his *Senchakushū* is clear. He used the words 'give up,' 'shut,' 'desert,' and 'abandon' in connection with the Buddhas, sutras, bodhisattvas, and gods. Because of this, saints and gods have left our country and famine and pestilence have come. You have quoted from many sutras and told me what is right and what is wrong. I am now released from wrong views. Now I can see and hear things clearly.

"The peace of our country is wished for not only by the emperor but also by all the people. We should stop supporting the *icchantika*s at once and make offerings to other monks and nuns. If we eliminate the Pai-lang (Hakurō) and Lu-lin (Ryokurin) warriors from the Buddha ocean and the Dharma mountain, our country will be as peaceful as [China] in the reign of Fu-hsi (Fukki), Shen-nung (Shinnō), T'ang-yao (Tōgyō), or Y'u-shun (Gushun). Then we shall be able to fathom the profundity of the various teachings of the Buddha and to respect the most honorable leaders of Buddhism."

The Master delightedly says:

"A dove turns into a hawk, and a sparrow transforms itself into a clam. A mugwort plant straightens itself when it grows among the hemp plants. How glad I am! You have changed. If you think of [the cause of] the calamities seriously and believe my words, winds will abate, waves will subside, and there will soon be a good harvest. But the mind changes as time passes. A thing changes its nature according to its circumstances. The reflection of the moon on the water is moved by the waves. The soldiers at the front withdraw when they see the swords of the enemy. Now you believe what I say, but you will soon forget it. If you wish for peace in our country during and after your present life, you should lose no time in eliminating [those who slander the Right Dharma].

The reason for this is as follows. Five of the seven calamities foretold in the *Yakushikyō* have already taken place. The remaining two are foreign invasions and rebellions in our country. Two of the three disasters predicted in the *Daijikkyō* have already appeared. The remaining one is the disaster of war. Many calamities that are prophesied in the *Konkōmyōkyō* have already occurred, except for invasions by the armies of surrounding countries. Six of the seven calamities predicted in the *Ninnōkyō* have already taken place. The remaining one is invasion by the armies of surrounding countries. The same sutra also says that when a country is thrown into disorder, devils will become active. When devils become active, all the country will go wild. If we look at present
208a conditions [in our country] in the light of these passages, we can say this: Many devils are active, and many people have died. Predictions about calamities have turned out to be true. Is it not certain that the remaining calamities will take place? What can we do when those remaining calamities come about because of our belief in wrong teachings?

"The king rules the people for the benefit of the country, and the people also work for that benefit. The people will be shocked and confused if the army of another country invades their country and rebels occupy part of the territory of that country. Where can we go if our country is destroyed and our houses are lost? If you want to have peace for yourself, you should first pray for the peace of our country.

"People fear that they may fall into [the evil realms] in a future life. Thus they believe wrong teachings and respect slanderers of the

Right Dharma. They are to be blamed because they do not know right from wrong, but they are to be pitied because they want to take refuge in the teachings of the Buddha in some way. If they have faith in the Buddha at all, they should not believe wrong teachings. If they do not change their minds and continue clinging [to wrong teachings], they will fall into the Hell of Incessant Suffering in their future lives.

"The reason for that is explained by the Buddha in the *Daijikkyō:*

> Suppose there lives a king who practiced almsgiving, kept the precepts, and made efforts to obtain wisdom in his innumerable previous existences. Now he sees my teaching being destroyed. If he does not protect it, all the innumerable roots of goodness he planted [in his previous existences] will perish.... The king will become seriously ill before long, and will be reborn in a great hell after his death.... The same will happen to his queen, crown prince, ministers, headmen of cities and villages, generals, governors of counties, and prime ministers.

"The *Ninnōkyō* says:

> Anyone who destroys the teaching of the Buddha will have no filial child. He will feud with his relatives. He will not be protected by gods. He will be visited by pestilence and devils every day. He will have many fears and difficulties throughout his life. After he dies, he will fall into three evil realms, the realms of hell, hungry ghosts, or animals. When he is reborn in the world of humans, he will be the servant of a soldier. He will have to incur retribution in this triple world as surely as a sound is accompanied by an echo or as the figure of a person is followed by a shadow or as the letters written in the night remain intact even when the light is out.

"The *Saddharmapuṇḍarīka-sūtra,* Volume II, says, 'Those who do not believe this sutra and slander it...will fall into the Avīci Hell when their present life ends.'

"In the Sadāparibhūta Bodhisattva chapter of the *Hokekyō,* Volume VII, the Buddha says, '[The four kinds of devotees at that time abused me with anger.] They will suffer much in the Avīci Hell for a thousand *kalpa*s.'

"The *Nehangyō* says:

> Those who avoid good friends, and who do not hear the Right Dharma...but cling to wrong teachings...will fall into the Avīci Hell, where they will undergo all the suffering to be found all over the area extending for eighty-four thousand square *yojana*s.

"Here we see that slandering the Right Dharma is the gravest sin. Alas! The people [of our country] have gone out of the gate of the Right Dharma and entered the hell of wrong teachings. How foolish! They are bound by the ropes of wrong teachings and caught by the net of slandering the Right Dharma. They are blinded by the mist [of wrong teaching] and sunk deep into the flames [of
208b hell]. How lamentable! How terrible! You should immediately convert to faith in the Good Dharma of the True Vehicle. Then the triple world will become a Buddha land. How can a Buddha land decline? The worlds of the ten directions will become a treasure world. How can a treasure world be destroyed?

"If our country does not decline and is not destroyed, we will be safe and peaceful. Believe my words, treasure them!"

Response of the Traveler

The traveler says:

"Everyone is eager for peace not only in his present life but also in his future lives. Having heard from you the words of the Buddha given in those sutras, I understand that slandering the Right Dharma is the gravest sin. I believed in a particular Buddha and abandoned all the other Buddhas. I respected the three sutras [of the Jōdo school] and deserted all the other sutras. I did all this according to the advice of the leaders [of the Jōdo school], not according to my own opinion. I think that other people in the ten directions are also like me. There is no doubt that we shall exhaust our minds in vain during our present life and fall into the Avīci Hell in our future lives if we do all this. Having heard your compassionate words, I have had my ignorant mind enlightened. I will do my best to eliminate [slanderers of the Right Dharma] so that our country may be peaceful. May I have peace not only in my present life but also in my future lives. I will not only enjoy my belief in [the Right Dharma], but also correct the mistakes of other people."

KANJINHONZONSHŌ

Translator's Introduction

The original title of this text, *Nyoraimetsugogogohyakusaishikanjinhonzonshō,* is usually shortened to *Kanjinhonzonshō*. Nichiren wrote this treatise on April 25, 1273, during his exile at Ichinosawa on Sado Island.

Nichiren's intention in this text was to reveal the Most Venerable One as he conceived of it. He describes the true object of worship on page 92 of this translation. According to Nichiren, the stupa of Prabhūtaratna Buddha hangs in the sky. In the center of the stupa exist the Five Characters (more properly, seven characters with the addition of the honorific *"Namu"*): *Myōhō Renge Kyō*. To Nichiren, *Myōhō Renge Kyō* is not only the name of the *Lotus Sutra* but also the name of the Dharma expounded in that sutra. On each side of the *Myōhō Renge Kyō* sit the two Buddhas, Śākyamuni and Prabhūtaratna. There are innumerable bodhisattvas sitting on their thrones in the sky below the stupa. All these bodhisattvas are followers of Śākyamuni Buddha. The four bodhisattvas Viśiṣṭacāritra, Anantacāritra, Viśuddhacāritra, and Supratiṣṭhitacāritra occupy the highest seats. These four bodhisattvas represent the four disciples of Śākyamuni who followed him when he attained enlightenment in the remote past. They are known as the leading disciples of the Original Śākyamuni Buddha. The four bodhisattvas Mañjuśrī, Samantabhadra, Maitreya, and Bhaiṣajyarāja occupy the second-highest seats. They represent the disciples of Śākyamuni who followed him when he displayed his attainment of enlightenment at Bodh Gayā. They are called the leading disciples of the Historical Śākyamuni Buddha. All the other bodhisattvas, who are the disciples either of Śākyamuni Buddha or of the Buddhas of the other worlds, occcupy the lowest seats. The Buddhas of the worlds of the ten directions sit on the ground, showing that they are emanations of the Original Śākyamuni Buddha.

From this description, it would appear that the *Myōhō Renge Kyō* is regarded as the Most Venerable One. Śākyamuni Buddha, who is held to be the Original Buddha of the other Buddhas, is placed on the left side of Prabhūtaratna Buddha. In Buddhist iconography, the left side is lower than the right side in status. The juxtaposition of two Buddhas is one of the characteristics of the *Lotus Sutra*. Whenever two Buddhas sit side by side in a Buddhist pictorial or sculptural image, we immediately know that the representation shows the influence of the *Lotus Sutra*. However, the supremacy of Śākyamuni Buddha is vitiated when he is placed in a hierarchically lower position than another Buddha.

Nichiren, however, clearly uses the expression "the Buddha revealed in the 'Chapter on the Duration of the Life of the Tathāgata' as a synonym for the Most Venerable One in a passage on page 93. This tells us that the Most Venerable One described on the preceding page is Śākyamuni Buddha, not the *Myōhō Renge Kyō*.

According to Chapter XI of the *Lotus Sutra,* Prabhūtaratna Buddha is a past Buddha who lived innumerable *kalpa*s ago in a Ratnaviśuddhā world located at a distance of innumerable worlds to the east of the Sāha world, which corresponds to our world. He vowed to praise any Buddha who would expound the *Lotus Sutra*. He held that the *Lotus Sutra* should be expounded by a Buddha who would emanate the Buddhas of the worlds of the ten directions from himself so that the validity of the sutra might be universally known. He made a stupa and instructed his disciples that after his *parinirvāṇa* they were to position his body into the meditation posture and place it in the stupa so that he could wait for an opportunity to hear a Buddha expound the *Lotus Sutra*.

Innumerable *kalpa*s later, Śākyamuni Buddha appeared in the Sāha world. He expounded the first ten chapters of the *Lotus Sutra,* and then announced that the Buddhas of the worlds of the ten directions were, in fact, his emanations, that he had dispatched them from the Sāha world to those worlds, and that he had supernatural power to call them back to the Sāha world.

Hearing this, Prabhūtaratna rejoiced and caused his stupa to travel westward through the skies under the innumerable worlds. The stupa reached the sky under the Sāha world and went up through the earth to a spot in the air facing Mount Gṛdhrakūṭa. Prabhūtaratna praised Śākyamuni from within the stupa. The congregation asked Śākyamuni to open the door of the stupa. Prabhūtaratna said that Śākyamuni would be allowed to open the door of the stupa if the Buddhas of the worlds of the ten directions assembled in the Sāha world. Śākyamuni collected the Buddhas, opened the door of the stupa, and entered the stūpa at Prabhūtaratna's request. Prabhūtaratna took the right seat because he was a past Buddha. Śākyamuni let him do so because at that time he was still behaving as a present Buddha, not as the Original Buddha of all past, present, and future Buddhas.

In Chapter XVI of the *Lotus Sutra,* Śākyamuni announced that he was the Original Buddha not only of the Buddhas of the worlds of the ten directions but also of the Buddhas of the past, present, and future. Here it was disclosed that Prabhūtaratna was one of the followers of the Original Śākyamuni Buddha, as Nichiren stated in the *Hokkeshuyōshō*. But the position of Prabhūtaratna in the stupa did not change even after this announcement. Nichiren was by no means a monotheist as conceived in Western theology. He instructed his followers to worship the "three Buddhas"—Śākyamuni, Prabhūtaratna, and the Buddhas of the worlds of the ten directions—and to pray to them for their protection. Theoretically, Prabhūtaratna was one of the past Buddhas who emanated from the Original Śākyamuni Buddha, but practically he was treated as a trustworthy witness to Śākyamuni, or as a ratifier of the sovereignty of the King of the Dharma. To Nichiren, Prabhūtaratna was a living presence who actively assisted him. Nichiren was convinced that the peace and integrity of the kingdom of the Dharma was guaranteed by Prabhūtaratna and safeguarded by the Buddhas of the worlds of the ten directions.

The *Myōhō Renge Kyō* is, Nichiren says, the name of the Dharma itself. He identifies it with the good medicine mentioned in the parable of an excellent physician in Chapter XVI of the *Lotus Sutra*. He goes on to say that the *Myōhō Renge Kyō* is the seed of Buddhahood that should be sown in the minds of people who live in the Age of Degeneration.

Buddhists of Nichiren's time believed that the Buddha lived from 1029 to 949 B.C.E. The theory of the three periods of the Buddha's teaching held that the first millennium after the Buddha's *parinirvāṇa* was the Age of the Right Teachings of the Buddha, the second millennium was the Age of the Counterfeit of the Right Teachings of the Buddha, and the following ten millenniums made up the Age of Degeneration. According to this theory, many people are able to attain enlightenment during the first five centuries after the Buddha's *parinirvāṇa;* during the second five centuries many are able to practice meditation but few attain enlightenment; during the third five centuries many study sutras but few practice meditation; during the fourth five centuries many build temples but few study sutras; and during the fifth five centuries people quarrel with each other and there is no possibility of studying or practicing Buddhism. Nichiren believed that he was living in the Age of Degeneration and also in the Age of Conflicts, and that this was the time to propagate the *Lotus Sutra* to sow the seed of Buddhahood in the minds of people.

Nichiren's description of the Most Venerable One on page 92 can be interpreted in the following way. The Most Venerable One is Śākyamuni Buddha. When he entered the stupa of Prabhūtaratna, the stupa changed into the palace of the King of the Dharma. Prabhūtaratna was treated as a reliable colleague of Śākyamuni. On the roof of the palace is hoisted the banner of the Five Characters, which served as the royal standard. Where there is the banner, there lives the Original Śākyamuni Buddha. Without the banner, the Original Śākyamuni Buddha does not live there, no matter how magnificent the palace may be.

In Nichiren's time, social unrest in Japan was increasingly prevalent. Recognizing that the political power of the imperial family was still too strong for the Kamakura regime to wrest control of the whole country, the Kamakura government attempted to compromise with the Kyoto regime by importing noblemen and princes as shoguns. The Kyoto regime itself was split into two houses which would later develop into the Two Dynasties. A Mongol invasion was imminent. The warrior-monks of Mount Hiei were constantly fighting with the military forces of Onjoji. Nichiren began propagating the *Lotus Sutra* in this warlike period, and it can be said that Nichiren's conception of the Most Venerable One reflected the militant trend of the time.

The "Great Mandala," said to have been written by Nichiren on July 8, 1275, was basically a representation of the Most Venerable One described on page 92 of this translation of the *Kanjinhonzonshō*.

A Note on the Translation

Except for the *Lotus Sutra,* which is referred to in both Sanskrit (*Saddharmapuṇḍarīka-sūtra*) and romanized Japanese (*Hokekyō*), the names of Buddhist texts quoted in this work appear in romanized Japanese; the original Sanskrit (where applicable) and/or romanized Chinese title is given on first appearance, along with the title in English. The names of Chinese figures and dynasties are given in romanized Chinese, followed by their romanized Japanese equivalent on first appearance.

KANJINHONZONSHŌ

OR

THE MOST VENERABLE ONE REVEALED BY INTROSPECTING OUR MINDS FOR THE FIRST TIME AT THE BEGINNING OF THE FIFTH OF THE FIVE FIVE HUNDRED-YEAR AGES

by

Nichiren, Śrāmaṇa of Japan

The *Makashikan,* Volume V, says:

> One mind contains ten realms within itself. Each realm also contains ten realms within itself. Therefore, there are one hundred realms altogether in one mind. Each realm has thirty things. Therefore, there are three thousand things in one hundred realms. (Things include suchnesses.) These three thousand things are in one mind. Where there is no mind, there is nothing. Where there is mind at all, there are three thousand things altogether therein.... That is why one mind is called an area beyond our comprehension. This is what I mean to say. 272a

(Another text of the *Makashikan* states, "There are three phases of existence in one realm.")

Question: Is there any mention of one mind–three thousand in the *Hokkegengi* (*Fa hua hsüan i; Profound Meaning of the Lotus*)?

Answer: Miao-le (Myōraku) denied it.

Question: Is there any mention of one mind–three thousand in the *Hokkemongu* (*Fa hua wen chu; Phrases from the Dharma Flower*)?

Answer: Miao-le denied it.

Question: What did he say?

Answer: He said, "One mind–three thousand has not yet been mentioned in those books."

Question: Is there any mention of one mind–three thousand in the first four volumes of the *Makashikan,* [which is composed of ten volumes]?

Answer: Miao-le denied it.

Question: What did he say?

Answer: He said:

> Therefore, one mind–three thousand was for the first time introduced in [Volume V], where the way of observing the Dharma was dealt with, and the teaching of one mind–three thousand was established as the fundamental principle [for the way of observing the Dharma].

Here we have a problem. The *Hokkegengi,* Volume II, says:

> One realm contains nine other realms within itself. [One realm has ten suchnesses. Because there are one hundred realms altogether,] one hundred realms have one thousand suchnesses altogether.

The *Hokkemongu,* Volume I, says:

> One sense organ or sense object contains ten realms within itself. Each realm contains ten realms. [Therefore, there are one hundred realms altogether.] One realm has ten suchnesses. Therefore, there are one thousand suchnesses altogether.

The *Kannongengi* (*Kuan-yin hsüan i; Profound Meaning of Kannon*) says:

> Ten realms interpenetrate one another. Therefore, there are one hundred realms altogether. Ten suchnesses such as nature and appearance are latent in one mind. Although these ten suchnesses are not manifest, they exist in one mind as ever.

[These statements show that the teaching of one mind–three thousand has already been expounded before the *Makashikan,* although partially.]

Question: Is there any mention of one mind–three thousand in the first four volumes of the *Makashikan*?

Answer: Miao-le denied it.

Question: What did he say?

Answer: He said in the *Shikanguketsu* (*Chih kuan hung chüeh*), Volume V:

> [Observing the Dharma is also expressed as practicing the Dharma. Practicing the Dharma requires understanding the Dharma. There are two sections in the *Makashikan:* the section of understanding the Dharma and the section of practicing the Dharma. The first six chapters, which cover the first four volumes, deal with understanding the Dharma, while Chapter VII, "Right Observation," which covers the last six volumes, treats practicing the Dharma. It seems that the "Chapter on Expedients," which occupies Volume IV, belongs to the section of practicing the Dharma because it deals with twenty-five expedients of understanding the Dharma, the expedients necessary for practicing the Dharma, but] comparing it to [Chapter VII on] "Right Observation," we cannot say that [Chapter VI on "Expedients"] deals with practicing the Dharma [because Chapter VI] deals with twenty-five expedients [of understanding the Dharma, the expedients necessary for practicing the Dharma], not with the proper way of practicing the Dharma. Therefore, we should say that the first six chapters belong to [the section of] understanding the Dharma.... Therefore, it can be said that one mind—three thousand was for the first time introduced in [Volume V,] where the way of observing the Dharma was first dealt with, and that the teaching of one mind—three thousand was established as the fundamental principle [for the way of observing the Dharma. The teaching of one mind—three thousand] is [T'ien-t'ai Chih-i Ta- 272b
> shih's] final and utmost teaching. [Chang-an (Sho-an) Tashih] said in his Preface [to the *Makashikan*], "[T'ien-t'ai] expounded what he had practiced in his mind." He was right

> in saying this. Those who read the *Makashikan* should not think otherwise.

[Tien-t'ai] Chih-i propagated the Dharma for thirty years. During the first twenty-nine years he expounded the *Hokkegengi, Hokkemongu,* and other texts, and established the five periods of the Buddha's teaching, the eight kinds of the Buddha's teaching, and the teaching of one thousand suchnesses in one hundred realms. He criticized wrong views of Chinese Buddhist teachers who had lived during five hundred and more years prior to him. His theories had never been established by any Buddhist philosophers in India. Chang-an Ta-shih says:

> Even the great *śāstra*s of Indian Buddhist philosophers are incomparably of less value than the works of T'ien-t'ai. It is needless to say of the works of the other Chinese teachers. This is no exaggeration. You can see this when you compare their teachings with each other.

The teaching of one mind—three thousand is the treasure of the Tendai school. The founders of the Kegon and Shingon schools took this treasure from the Tendai school. Alas! Without knowing this fact, many followers of T'ien-t'ai have affiliated themselves with the Kegon or Shingon schools. Chang-an Ta-shih feared that such an appropriation might occur in the future, saying, "It will be lamentable if the expounder of the teaching of one mind—three thousand is forgotten."

Question: What is the difference between the teaching of one thousand suchnesses in one hundred realms and the teaching of one mind—three thousand?

Answer: The teaching of one thousand suchnesses in one hundred realms concerns only sentient beings, while the teaching of one mind—three thousand is related to all beings, sentient or nonsentient.

Question: If you admit that non-sentient beings also have ten suchnesses, you must say that plants possess mind and that plants also will become Buddhas just like sentient beings. Do you mean to say this?

Answer: This is very difficult to believe and very difficult to understand.

T'ien-t'ai says that there are two things difficult to believe and difficult to understand: 1) contradictory statements in sutras, and 2) the philosophy of the *Saddharmapuṇḍarīka-sūtra*.

We find contradictory statements in sutras. The sutras expounded before the *Saddharmapuṇḍarīka-sūtra* have the following two statements: 1) adherents of the two vehicles and *icchantikas* can never become Buddhas, and 2) the Lord Teacher Śākyamuni, the World-honored One, attained enlightenment during his historical life. The first statement is denied in the first fourteen chapters of the *Saddharmapuṇḍarīka-sūtra,* and the second statement is disproved in the second fourteen chapters of the same sutra. Statements of the same Buddha are sometimes as different from each other as water is from fire. Who can believe these contradictory statements? This is one of the things difficult to believe and difficult to understand.

According to the philosophy of the *Saddharmapuṇḍarīka-sūtra,* one hundred realms have each ten suchnesses. There are three thousand things in one mind. Therefore, non-sentient beings also have mind. Since they have mind, they have ten suchnesses. This is the other thing difficult to believe and difficult to understand.

In Buddhist sutras and also in non-Buddhist scriptures, a wooden image or [painted] picture is claimed to represent the Most Venerable One. A wooden image or picture is made from plants, which are non-sentient beings. The use of a non-sentient being to represent the Most Venerable One is justified only by the teaching of the Tendai school. It is useless to worship a wooden image or picture of the Most Venerable One if plants have no mind, in other words, if plants have not ten suchnesses such as cause and effect.

Question: In what text does it say that plants and lands (countries) have ten suchnesses such as cause and effect?

Answer: It says in the *Makashikan,* Volume V, "A country also has ten suchnesses. An evil country has an evil appearance, an evil nature, an evil entity, an evil power...." It says in the *Gengishakusen* (*Hsüan i shih ch'ien*), Volume VI:

> [Ten suchnesses can be classified into two headings: matter and mind.] Appearance is matter. Nature is mind. Entity, power, activity, and environmental cause are matter and mind. Primary cause and effect are mind. Rewards and retributions are matter.

It says in the *Kombeiron* (*Chin pei lun; Golden Spirit Treatise*):

272c

> Even a [blade of] grass, a tree, a pebble, or a particle of dust possess Buddha-nature. It has ten suchnesses such as cause and effect, and has wisdom and practice enough to develop its Buddha-nature into Buddhahood.

Question: I understand the textual sources. [Now I have noticed that in T'ien-t'ai's works, "observing the Dharma" is sometimes expressed as "introspecting the mind."] What do you mean by "introspecting the mind"?

Answer: "To introspect the mind" means to see ten realms in our own minds. I can see the six sense organs of others, but I cannot see my own six sense organs unless I look at myself in a mirror. The six realms and the four kinds of saints (Buddhas, bodhisattvas, *pratyekabuddha*s, and *śrāvaka*s) are mentioned in many sutras, but I cannot see ten realms, one hundred realms, one thousand suchnesses, and three thousand things in my mind unless I look at myself in the mirror of the *Saddharmapuṇḍarīka-sūtra,* the *Makashikan,* and other writings of T'ien-t'ai [Chih-i] Ta-shih.

Question: What does it say in the *Saddharmapuṇḍarīka-sūtra* in connection with these teachings? How does T'ien-t'ai comment on the words of the sutra?

Answer: [Living beings are of ten kinds: Buddhas, bodhisattvas, *pratyekabuddha*s, *śrāvaka*s, *deva*s, humans, *asura*s, animals, hungry ghosts, and hell beings. They live in ten different realms. The realm of the *deva*s is called heaven.] The Buddha says in the "Chapter on Expedients" in the *Saddharmapuṇḍarīka-sūtra,* Volume I, "[The Buddhas appear in the worlds] in order to cause all living beings to open the gate to the insight of the Buddhas." This shows that the realm of Buddhas exists in the nine other realms.

The Buddha says in the "Chapter on the Duration of the Life of the Tathāgata" in the same sutra:

> As I said before, it is a very long time since I became the Buddha. The duration of my life is innumerable *asaṃkhya kalpa*s. I am always here. I shall never pass away. Good men! The duration of my life, which I obtained by my practice of the Way of bodhisattvas, has not yet expired. It is twice as long as the length of time previously stated.

This shows that the realm of Buddhas contains the nine other realms.

It says in the same sutra, "Devadatta will become a Buddha...called Heavenly King Tathāgata." This shows that the realm of Buddhas exists in the realm of hell.

It says in the same sutra:

> There are [*rākṣasī*s called] Lambā.... Your merits will be immeasurable even when you protect anyone who keeps only the name of the *Saddharmapuṇḍarīka-sūtra.*

This shows that the ten realms exist in the realm of hungry ghosts.

It says in the same sutra, "The daughter of the dragon king...attained perfect enlightenment." This shows that the ten realms exist in the realm of animals.

The Buddha says in the same sutra:

> [Medicine King! Do you see the innumerable *devas*...and *asuras* including] Balin Asura King [. . .in this great multitude? If in my presence any of them rejoices even on a moment's thought,] at hearing even a *gāthā* or a phrase [of the *Saddharmapuṇḍarīka-sūtra,* I will assure him of his future Buddhahood, saying to him, "You] will be able to attain *anuttara-samyak-saṃbodhi.*"

This shows that the ten realms exist in the realm of the *asuras*.

The Buddha says in the same sutra, "Those [who carved an image of the Buddha. . .] in his honor, have already attained the enlightenment of the Buddha." This shows that the ten realms exist in the realm of humans.

Great Brahmā Heavenly King [and other gods] say in the same sutra, "We also shall be able to become Buddhas." This shows that the ten realms exist in heaven (the realm of *devas*).

The Buddha says to Śāriputra in the same sutra, "You will be able to. . .become a Buddha called Flower Light Tathāgata." This shows that the ten realms exist in the realm of *śrāvakas*.

It says in the same sutra:

> Those who are seeking the vehicle of the cause-knowers, and the *bhikṣus* and *bhikṣuṇīs*. . .are joining their hands together respectfully, wishing to hear the Perfect Way.

This shows that the ten realms exist in the realm of *pratyekabuddhas*.

It says in the same sutra:

> Thereupon the bodhisattva *mahāsattvas* as numerous as the particles of dust of one thousand worlds who had sprung up from underground. . .[said to the Buddha, "We also wish to obtain] this true, pure, and great Dharma."

This shows that the ten realms exist in the realm of bodhisattvas.

The Buddha says in the same sutra:

> I told the stories of my previous lives [in some sutras] and the stories of the previous lives of other Buddhas [in other 273a
> sutras].

This shows that the ten realms exist in the realm of Buddhas.

Question: I can see the six sense organs of others. I also can see those of my own [when I look at myself in a mirror]. But I cannot see the ten realms in myself or others. How can I believe it?

Answer: It says in the "Chapter on the Teacher of Dharma" in the *Saddharmapuṇḍarīka-sūtra,* "[The *Saddharmapuṇḍarīka-sūtra* is] the most difficult to believe and the most difficult to understand." It says in the "Chapter on Beholding the Stupa of Treasures":

> It is not difficult to expound all the other sutras.... It is not difficult to grasp Mount Sumeru.... It is not difficult to move a world.... It is not difficult to stand in the highest heaven.... It is difficult to expound this sutra.... It is not difficult to grasp the sky.... It is difficult to copy and keep this sutra.... It is not difficult to put the great earth on the nail of a toe.... It is difficult to read this sutra.... It is not difficult to shoulder a load of hay and stay unburned in the fire.... It is difficult to keep this sutra.... It is not difficult to keep the storehouse of eighty-four thousand teachings.... It is difficult to hear and receive this sutra.... It is not difficult to expound the Dharma to many...living beings...so that they may be able to obtain the benefits [of] arhatship and the six supernatural powers. It is difficult to keep this sutra after my nirvana.

Here the expression "It is not difficult" is repeated nine times; and the expression "It is difficult" six times. We call this quotation] "the statement of the six difficulties and the nine easinesses."

T'ien-t'ai [Chih-i] Ta-shih says:

> [The *Saddharmapuṇḍarīka-sūtra*] is the most difficult to believe and the most difficult to understand because both the "Discourse of the Historical Buddha" and the "Discourse of the Eternal Buddha" in the sutra contradict the sutras expounded earlier.

Chang-an Ta-shih says:

> The Buddha says in this sutra, "[The Buddhas . . . appear in the worlds in order to cause all living beings to open the gate to the insight of the Buddha....] This is the one great purpose [for which the Buddhas appear in the worlds.]" It is no wonder that this sutra is not easy to understand.

Dengyō Daishi says:

> This *Saddharmapuṇḍarīka-sūtra* is the most difficult to believe and the most difficult to understand because the Buddha expounded this sutra without taking others' capacity for understanding into consideration.

Those who heard the Dharma directly from the Buddha (i.e., *śrāvaka*s) had already been given the roots of goodness in their previous existences. Furthermore, they were helped in understanding the Dharma by the Lord Teacher Śākyamuni, the World-honored One, Prabhūtaratna Buddha, the Replica-Buddhas of the worlds of the ten directions, the bodhisattvas as numerous as the particles of dust of one thousand worlds who had sprung up from underground, Mañjuśrī, Maitreya, and others. Yet some of them could not understand the Dharma.

[It says in the *Saddharmapuṇḍarīka-sūtra:*

> When the Buddha said this,] five thousand people [among the *bhikṣu*s, *bhikṣuṇī*s, *upāsaka*s, and *upāsikā*s (i.e., the four kinds of devotees) of this congregation rose from their seats . . . and] retired.

[It says in the same sutra,] "Gods and humans were removed to other worlds [except those who were in the congregation.]"

[The above two quotations show that even in the lifetime of the Buddha some people could not believe the Dharma.] Needless to say, the people who lived in the Age of the Right Teachings of the Buddha and the Age of the Counterfeit of the Right Teachings of the Buddha could not believe it. Neither can the people who are now living at the beginning of the Age of Degeneration. The Dharma that you say is easy to believe may not be the Right Dharma.

Question: I understand the meaning of the quotations from the sutra and from the works of T'ien-t'ai and Chang-an. But I cannot believe those contradicatory statements in sutras even though they were stated by the Buddha himself. Those contradictory statements are as if to say that fire is water or that black is white. I can see only human beings when I look at the faces of others. I can see only a human being when I look at my face in a mirror. How can I believe [that the realm of humans contains the ten realms]?

Answer: When you see others, you will find that they are sometimes happy and at other times angry, peaceful, greedy, foolish, or flattering. When they are angry, they are in hell. When they are greedy, they are hungry ghosts. When they are foolish, they are animals. When they are flattering, they are *asuras*. When they are happy, they are in heaven. When they are peaceful, they are human beings. Here you can see the six realms in the faces of others. The four kinds of saints are not conspicuous in their faces, but you can find them if you observe the faces of others carefully.

Question: It seems that the six realms exist in others' faces as you say even though they are not so clear. But I cannot find the four kinds of saints there at all. Can you find them?

Answer: A moment ago you said that you could see only humans in others' faces. Now you say that it seems that the six realms exist in others' faces. I think you will say pretty soon that the four kinds of saints also exist in others' faces. I will try to make some comments.

Nothing is permanent in this world. I know that some people realize this truth. Here we can say that they are adherents of the two vehicles. Even the most cruel man loves his wife and child. He has part of bodhisattvahood.

As regards the realm of Buddhas, I must confess that it is not manifest in the realm of human beings. However, you should have no doubt that the realm of Buddhas also exists in the realm of humans because you have already realized that the nine other realms exist in the realm of humans. The Buddha says in the *Hokekyō* in regard to the realm of humans, "The Buddhas appear in the worlds in order to cause all living beings to open the gate to the insight of the Buddha." It says in the *Mahāparinirvāṇa-sūtra* (*Great Nirvana Sutra*), "The natural eyes of those who study the Great Vehicle can be called the eyes of the Buddha." The fact that ordinary humans can believe in the *Saddharmapuṇḍarīka-sūtra* even though they were born in the Age of Degeneration shows that the realm of humans contains the realm of Buddhas.

273b *Question:* I understand that the Buddha clearly states that the ten realms interpenetrate each other. But it is very difficult to believe that the realm of Buddhas exists in our minds filled with illusions. If I do not believe this I shall have to become an *icchantika*. Please let me believe this and save me from the Hell of Incessant Suffering out of your great compassion toward me.

Answer: You have already heard of the Buddha's statement regarding his sole purpose of appearing in this world. You must believe this because it is the words of the Buddha. If you do not believe in Śākyamuni, the World-honored One, who else can save you? Even the four kinds of reliable bodhisattvas cannot save you. Needless to say, we who live in the Age of Degeneration and have the Buddha-nature only in theory cannot save you.

However, I will try to say something [of the realm of Buddhas in our minds]. Some people who saw the Buddha directly did not attain enlightenment. They attained enlightenment when they saw Ānanda and others. There were two kinds of people: those who attained enlightenment by hearing the *Saddharmapuṇḍarīka-sūtra* directly from the Buddha and those who attained enlightenment by hearing the *Saddharmapuṇḍarīka-sūtra* not from the Buddha.

Before the rise of Buddhism, some brahmans in India obtained the right view of the Buddha through the teachings of the four Vedas. [Before Buddhism was introduced into China,] some Confucians or Taoists obtained the right view of the Buddha through the teachings of Confucianism.

[According to the "Discourse of the Historical Buddha" in the *Saddharmapuṇḍarīka-sūtra,*] Mahābhijñājñānābhibhū Buddha gave the seed of Buddhahood to living beings three thousand worlds dust particles *kalpa*s ago. [According to the "Discourse of the Original Buddha" in the same sutra,] the Original Śākyamuni Buddha gave the seed of Buddhahood to living beings five hundred thousand billion worlds dust particles *kalpa*s ago. [Before the *Saddharmapuṇḍarīka-sūtra,*] the Buddha expounded many Mahayana sutras during the Avataṃsaka, Vaipulya, and Prajñāpāramitā periods of his teaching. During these periods, many wise bodhisattvas and ordinary humans heard these Mahayana sutras and developed their seeds of Buddhahood.

Even after the rise of Buddhism, some people attained enlightenment without the direct teaching of the Buddha. For instance, *pratyekabuddha*s attained enlightenment by observing flying flowers and falling leaves.

Some Buddhist teachers today were not given the seed of Buddhahood in their previous existences. They cling to the teachings of the Hinayana or the Provisional Mahayana. They do not go beyond the views of the Hinayana or the Provisional Mahayana even after they encounter the *Saddharmapuṇḍarīka-sūtra.* Because they think their views are right, they say that the *Saddharmapuṇḍarīka-sūtra* is equal in value to Hinayana sutras, to the *Avataṃsaka-sūtra* (*Flower Ornament Sutra*), or to the *Mahāvairocana-sūtra,* or that the *Saddharmapuṇḍarīka-sūtra* is of less value than those sutras.

Such Buddhist teachers are inferior to the saints and sages of Confucianism and Brahmanism. I will stop comparing them with each other for now.

Let us go back to the teaching that the ten realms interpenetrate each other. It is as difficult [to believe this as it is] to believe that fire exists in stone or that flowers exist in a tree. But a flint produces fire and a tree blooms. The teaching that the realm of humans contains the realm of Buddhas is the most difficult to believe just as if to say that fire exists in water or that water exists in fire. But the dragon-fire comes out of water, and the dragon-water comes out of fire. It is unbelievable, but it is a fact. You have already accepted that the realm of humans contains the eight other realms. Why do you not believe that the only one remaining realm, the realm of Buddhas, exists also in the realm of humans? [Chinese] saints such as Yao-wang (Gyō-ō) and Shun-wang (Shun-ō) were impartial to their subjects. They were like Buddhas. Never Despising Bodhisattva saw a Buddha in the person whom he met. Crown Prince Siddhārtha became the Buddha. Judging from these facts, you should believe that the realm of Buddhas exists in the realm of humans.

Question: (Do not tell others carelessly what I say from here on.) The Lord Teacher Śākyamuni, the World-honored One, eliminated the three kinds of illusions. He was the lord of the worlds of the ten directions. He was the lord of all bodhisattvas, adherents of the two vehicles, humans, *deva*s, and other living beings. When he walked, Brahmā Heavenly King accompanied him on his left side, and Śakra on his right side. He was followed by the four kinds of devotees and the eight kinds of supernatural beings. He was led by Vajra. Surrounded by these gods and humans, he expounded eighty-four thousand storehouses of teachings to all living beings in order to liberate them from suffering. How can it be that such a
273c Buddha lives in the minds of us ordinary human beings?

According to the "Discourse of the Historical Buddha" in the *Hokekyō,* and in other sutras expounded before the *Hokekyō,* Lord

Teacher Śākyamuni, the World-honored One, attained enlightenment during his historical life. In his previous existences, he was Crown Prince Mahādāna, Mānava Bodhisattva, King Śibi, and Prince Sattva.

[According to the Hinayana sutras,] in his previous existences, the Buddha benefited others and made offerings to seventy-five thousand Buddhas for the first *asaṃkhya kalpas*, seventy-six thousand Buddhas for the second *asaṃkhya kalpas*, and seventy-seven thousand Buddhas for the third *asaṃkhya kalpas*. [According to the Mahayana-cum-Hinayana sutras,] he benefited others for longer than *kalpas* as numerous as particles of dust. [According to a Specialized Mahayana sutra,] he performed the bodhisattva practices for innumerable *asaṃkhya kalpas*. [According to a Perfect Mahayana sutra,] he began to perform the bodhisattva practices when he aspired to enlightenment, and continued to perform them for *kalpas* as numerous as the particles of dust produced by smashing worlds more than three thousand great thousand [in number]. He performed all these practices for so many *kalpas* and has become Lord Teacher Śākyamuni, the World-honored One, of today. I cannot believe that the ability to perform all these bodhisattva practices exists in our minds, and that the realm of bodhisattvas exists in the realm of humans.

Now let us regard the Buddha after his enlightenment. During the first forty and more years, the Historical Lord Teacher Śākyamuni, the World-honored One, manifested himself variously according to his four kinds of teachings (the Hinayana teachings, the Mahayana-cum-Hinayana teachings, the Specialized Mahayana teachings, and the Perfect Mahayana teachings), and expounded the sutras before the *Saddharmapuṇḍarīka-sūtra,* the first fourteen chapters of the *Saddharmapuṇḍarīka-sūtra*, and the *Mahāparinirvāṇa-sūtra* to benefit all living beings.

In the *Avataṃsaka-sūtra,* he manifests himself as Vairocana Buddha sitting on the lotus flower throne in the center of the worlds of the ten directions. In the Āgama sutras, he reveals himself as a Buddha who has attained enlightenment by eliminating illusions with thirty-four activities of his mind. In the Vaipulya sutras, he is accompanied by many Buddhas. In the Prajñāpāramitā sutras, he is accompanied by one thousand Buddhas. In the *Mahāvairocana-sūtra,* he manifests himself with seven hundred and more honorable ones of the Garbhadhātu Mandala. In the *Sarvatathāgatatattvasaṃgraha* (*Adamantine Pinnacle Sutra*), he reveals himself with five hundred and more honorable ones of the Vajradhātu Mandala, that is to say, with twelve hundred and more honorable ones altogether. In the "Chapter on Beholding the Stupa of Treasures" in the *Saddharmapuṇḍarīka-sūtra,* he shows us his four bodies (the inferior *nirmāṇakāya,* the superior *nirmāṇakāya,* the *saṃbhogakāya,* and the *dharmakāya*) in the four kinds of worlds (the world of saints living with non-saints, the world of adherents of the two vehicles, the world of bodhisattvas, and the world of Buddhas).

The four bodies of the Buddha are also revealed in the *Mahāparinirvāṇa-sūtra*. According to this sutra, Hinayana Buddhists see the Buddha as being sixteen feet tall. [Here the Buddha shows his inferior *nirmāṇakāya*. To adherents of the Mahayana-cum-Hinayana,] the Buddha is sometimes sixteen feet tall and at other times taller than that. [Here the Buddha shows his superior *nirmāṇakāya*.] In the Specialized Mahayana, the Buddha is called Vairocana. [Here the Buddha shows his *saṃbhogakāya*. In the Perfect Mahayana,] the Buddha is regarded as being as vast as the sky. [Here he shows his *dharmakāya*.]

The Buddha entered *parinirvāṇa* at the age of eighty and left his *śarīra*s (relics) to benefit people who were to live during [the three ages to come:] the Age of the Right Teachings of the Buddha, the Age of the Counterfeit of the Right Teachings of the Buddha, and the Age of Degeneration.

According to the "Discourse of the Original Buddha" in the *Saddharmapuṇḍarīka-sūtra,* Lord Teacher Śākyamuni, the World-honored One, already attained enlightenment more than five myriad million dust particle *kalpa*s ago. He was a bodhisattva before that.

The Original Śākyamuni Buddha dispatched his Replica-Buddhas to the worlds of the ten directions, and let them propagate his sacred teachings to save living beings as numerous as particles of dust. Since then he has had many disciples, more numerous than those of the Historical Buddha, just as a great ocean is more volumious than a drop of water or a great mountain is larger than a particle of dust. A bodhisattva who is a disciple of the Original Śākyamuni Buddha is more virtuous than Mañjuśrī, Avalokiteśvara, and other bodhisattvas in the worlds of the ten directions who are mentioned in the "Discourse of the Historical Buddha" in the *Saddharmapuṇḍarīka-sūtra,* just as Śakra is more honorable than a monkey. [I cannot believe that the Original Buddha as such lives in our minds, and that the realm of Buddhas exists in the realm of humans.]

You say that the ten realms are contained in our minds. As I told you now, I cannot believe that the realm of Buddhas exists in our minds. As I told you before, I cannot believe that the realm of bodhisattvas exists in the realm of humans. The same can be said of the eight other realms.] Adherents of the two vehicles in the worlds of the ten directions have already eliminated illusions and attained arhatship. You say that not only Buddhas, bodhisattvas, and adherents of the two vehicles but also gods, such as the Brahmā Heavenly Kings, Śakra, the Sun God, the Moon God, and the four great heavenly kings; and humans, such as the four wheel-turning holy kings (*cakravrtins*); and all the other living beings in the worlds of the ten directions, including denizens of the great fire of the Hell of Incessant Suffering, exist in our minds. Do all these ten realms exist in our minds at one thought? Are they three thousand things in our minds? I cannot believe the teaching of one mind–three thousand even if it has been stated by the Buddha. I think that the teachings of the Buddha expounded in the sutras before the *Saddharmapuṇḍarīka-sūtra* are true. It says in the *Avataṃsaka-sūtra,* "The Buddha has finally eliminated all falsehood. He is as stainless as the sky." It says in the *Ninnōkyō,* "The Buddha has found the fountainhead of all illusions and eliminated

it. Now he has only wonderful wisdom." It says in the *Vajracchedikāprajñāpāramitā-sūtra* (*Diamond Sutra*), "The Buddha has only pure good." It says in Aśvaghoṣa's *Mahāyānaśraddhotpāda-śāstra (Discourse on the Awakening of Faith in the Mahayana),* "There is only one merit of purity in the *tathāgatagarbha.*" It says in the *Vijñaptimātratāsiddhi-śāstra (Demonstration of Con-*
274a *sciousness Only*) [written by followers] of Vasubandhu Bodhisattva:

> [Birth and death cannot be completely eliminated even when illusions and obstacles to knowledge are eliminated. There still remains a seed of transformation. Furthermore, even when you obtain wisdom without illusions, you must have birth and death in the earlier stage of wisdom where your seed of wisdom is still immature.] Only when you enter into a *samādhi* as indestructible as a diamond will you be able to obtain the perfect and purest consciousness, and your birth and death will automatically cease to exist because neither the seed of transformation nor the immature seed of wisdom is caused by this purest consciousness.

Now let us compare the *Saddharmapuṇḍarīka-sūtra* with the other sutras. The sutras expounded before the *Saddharmapuṇḍarīka-sūtra* are innumerable. The time spent for expounding these sutras was much longer than that spent for expounding the *Saddharmapuṇḍarīka-sūtra*. If the earlier sutras contradict the *Saddharmapuṇḍarīka-sūtra,* we should follow the earlier sutras.

Aśvaghoṣa was "the eleventh patriarch," according to the *Fuhōzōinnenden* (*Fu fa tsang yin yüan chüan; Patriarchal Lineage of the Transmitters of the Buddha-Dharma*). Vasubandhu wrote one thousand *śāstra*s. He was among the first of the four kinds of reliable bodhisattvas. But T'ien-t'ai was a petty priest in a remote country. He wrote no *śāstra*. How can I believe him?

I do not want to abandon many to pick up one, but if the *Saddharmapuṇḍarīka-sūtra* clearly states that the ten realms interpenetrate each other, that there are one thousand suchnesses in one hundred realms, and that there are three thousand things in our minds, I will feel no reluctance in following it. In what part of the sutra do you find these teachings? As if to disprove your statement, the Buddha says in the sutra, "I have eliminated all evils."

There is no mention of the ten realms interpenetrating each other in Vasubandhu's *Saddharmapuṇḍarīkopadeśa* (*Commentary on the Lotus Sutra*) or Sāramati's *Mahāyanottaratantra-śāstra-vyākhyā* (*Treatise on the Mahāyanottaratantra*), or in any of the works of the teachers of the three schools in Southern China, the seven schools in Northern China, and the priests of the seven temples of Nara in Japan.

These teachings were created by the prejudice of T'ien-t'ai and introduced to Japan only by Dengyō. Ch'ing-liang Kuo-shih (Shōryō Kokushi) says, "T'ien-t'ai was wrong." Huiyüan Fa-shih (Eon Hosshi) says, "T'ien-t'ai called the Hinayana 'the teachings of the Tripiṭaka.' This is confusing because the Mahayana also has its own Tripiṭaka." Ryōkō says, "T'ien-t'ai did not yet understand the meaning of the *Avataṃsaka-sūtra.*" Tokuichi says, "Alas! Chikō (Chih-che)! Whose disciple are you? The Buddha expounded [the Middle Way, which is] the last of the three periods of the Buddha's teaching, with his broad and long tongue. You slander it with your tongue shorter than three inches." Kōbō Daishi says, "The founders of Chinese schools took the word 'ghee' from the *Ropparamitsukyō* (*Liu po lo mi ching; Sutra of the Six Pāramitās*) and used it to decorate their own schools."

The teaching of one mind–three thousand is not found in any of the sutras of the Mahayana, Provisional or True, expounded by the Buddha. Nor is it found in the *śāstra*s of the four kinds of reliable bodhisattvas in India, nor in the works of priests in China or Japan. How can I believe it?

Answer: This is the most difficult question, indeed. In the first place, you should bear in mind that the differences between the *Hokekyō* and the other sutras are clearly stated in the *Saddharmapuṇḍarīka-sūtra*. The differences are: 1) The Buddha says only in the *Saddharmapuṇḍarīka-sūtra* that he has for the first time expounded his true teaching; 2) [Prabhūtaratna Buddha proved] the truthfulness of the *Saddharmapuṇḍarīka-sūtra,* and [the Replica-Buddhas did the same] with their broad and long tongues; 3) adherents of the two vehicles are assured of their Buddhahood only in the *Saddharmapuṇḍarīka-sūtra;* and 4) the originality of the Buddha is revealed for the first time in the *Hokekyō*.

As regards the silence of Indian Buddhist philosophers [on the teaching of one mind—three thousand], T'ien-t'ai [Chih-i] Ta-shih says:

> Vasubandhu and Nāgārjuna knew the teaching but did not propagate it. They provisionally chose different theories according to the needs of the time. However, scholars after them interpreted the views of the two philosophers with prejudice, and clung to one or the other. Eventually, controversies arose between the followers of Vasubandhu and those of Nāgārjuna. They each held their own views, and grossly violated the Way of the Saint.

Chang-an Ta-shih says:

> Even the great *sāstras* of Indian [Buddhist philosophers] are incomparably of less value [than the works of T'ien-t'ai] and, needless to say, of the works of the other Chinese teach-
> 274b ers. This is no exaggeration. You can see this when you compare their teachings with each other.

Vasubandhu, Nāgārjuna, Aśvaghoṣa, and Sāramati knew the teaching [of one mind—three thousand], but they did not propagate it because the time was not yet ripe for that. Chinese teachers before T'ien-t'ai knew part of the teaching or did not know it at all. Some Chinese teachers after T'ien-t'ai criticized him, but later followed him while others did not follow him at all.

[You are right in saying that the Buddha states in the *Saddharmapuṇḍarīka-sūtra,*] "I have eliminated all evils." This is just a repetition of the teaching expounded in the earlier sutras. The same sutra clearly reveals the interpenetration of the ten realms. For it says, "The Buddhas appear in the worlds in order to cause all living beings to open the gate to the insight of the Buddha."

T'ien-t'ai comments on this statement, saying:

> If living beings do not have the insight of the Buddha within themselves, they cannot open the gate to it. Know this! The insight of the Buddha is latent in the minds of living beings.

Chang-an Ta-shih says:

> If living beings do not have the insight of the Buddha within themselves, the Buddha cannot cause them to open the gate to it. [Suppose a poor woman does not know that she is the owner of a storehouse of treasures.] If the poor woman does not [actually] possess a storehouse of treasures, no one can show her the storehouse of treasures of her own.

[You say that you cannot believe that the Buddha lives in the minds of ordinary people, that the ability to perform the bodhisattva practices exists in our minds, that not only the realms of Buddhas and bodhisattvas but also the eight other realms exist in our minds at one thought, and that there are three thousand things in our minds.] It is very difficult to have you believe all this. The Buddha says in the *Saddharmapuṇḍarīka-sūtra:*

> I have expounded many sutras. I am now expounding this sutra. I will also expound many sutras in the future.... This sutra is the most difficult to believe and the most difficult to understand.

He goes on to say that this is the sutra of six difficulties while the other sutras are the sutras of nine easinesses, as previously stated.

T'ien-t'ai [Chih-i] Ta-shih says:

> The teachings expounded both in the "Discourse of the Historical Buddha" and the "Discourse of the Eternal Buddha"

> in the *Saddharmapuṇḍarīka-sūtra* are quite different from the teachings expounded in the earlier sutras. The teachings of the *Hokekyō* are the most difficult to believe and the most difficult to understand. The difficulty is as that experienced by a vanguard of an army.

Chang-an Ta-shih says, "The Buddha says that the interpenetration of the ten realms is the most important teaching. How can it be that it is easy to understand?"

Dengyō Daishi says:

> The *Saddharmapuṇḍarīka-sūtra* is the most difficult to believe and the most difficult to understand because it was expounded without taking the capacity of its hearers into consideration.

Only three persons in history knew this Great Dharma during one thousand eight hundred and more years after the *parinirvāṇa* of the Buddha throughout the three countries [of] India, China, and Japan. They were Śākyamuni, the World-honored One of India, [T'ien-t'ai] Chih-i Ta-shih of China, and Dengyō of Japan. They can be called the Three Sages of Buddhism.

Question: How about Nāgārjuna and Vasubandhu?

Answer: They knew it but did not propagate it. They propagated part of the teachings expounded in the first fourteen chapters of the *Saddharmapuṇḍarīka-sūtra* but did not speak of the teachings expounded in the rest of the sutra or of the way of introspecting our minds. In one case this was because the time was not yet ripe for that although there were hearers [who were capable of understanding these teachings], and in another case it was because there were no hearers capable of understanding them.

After T'ien-t'ai and Dengyō, many people knew this Right Dharma because the wisdom of these two saints was known. Teachers after T'ien-t'ai first opposed him and later followed him. They included Chia-hsiang (Kajō) of the Sanron school, one hundred and more priests of the three schools in Southern China and of the seven schools in Northern China; Fa-ts'ang (Hōzō), Ch'ing-liang, and others of the Kegon school, Hsüan-tsang San-ts'ang (Genjō Sanzō), T'ü-en Ta-shih (Jion Daishi), and others of the Hossō school; Śubhakarasiṃha San-ts'ang, Vajrabodhi San-ts'ang, Amoghavajra San-ts'ang, and others of the Shingon school; and Tao-hsien (Dōsen) and others of the Ritsu school.

Now I will answer your question [about the existence of the Buddha in our minds]. The Buddha addresses Great Adornment Bodhisattva Mahāsattva in the *Muryōgikyō* (*Wu liang i ching; Sutra of Infinite Meaning*):

> Suppose a prince was born to a king and queen. Then passed 274c
> one day, two days, seven days; one month, two months, seven months; one year, two years, seven years. Now the young prince was seven years old. Although he was not yet able to rule the country, the people respected him and the sons of great kings befriended him. The king and queen loved him and always enjoyed speaking with him because he was still immature.
>
> Good man! A bodhisattva who keeps this sutra will be like the young prince. The prince, who was a bodhisattva, had the Buddha as his father and this sutra as his mother. If he hears this sutra and recites even one phrase or verse of this sutra one time, two times, ten times, one hundred times, one thousand, times, one billion times, as many times as there are sands in the Ganges River, or innumerable, uncountable times, then he will be respected by all four kinds of devotees and the eight kinds of supernatural beings, will be accompanied by great bodhisattvas, and will be loved and protected by the Buddhas even though he does not yet understand the truth perfectly because he has just begun to study.

It says in the *Kanfugenbosatsugyōbōkyō* (*Kuan p'u hsien p'u sa hsing fa ching; Conduct of Meditation on Samantabhadra Sutra*):

> This sutra of the Great Vehicle is the treasure store of the Buddhas, the eyes of the Buddhas of the worlds of the ten directions in the past, present, and future, and the seed which gave, is giving, and will give birth to past, present, and future Buddhas....
>
> Practice the Great Vehicle lest the seed of Buddhahood be eliminated.... This Vaipulya sutra is the eyes of the Buddhas. The Buddhas were able to obtain the five kinds of eyes by this sutra. The *trikāyas* of the Buddha were caused by this sutra. This sutra is the seal of the Great Dharma, which confirms the sea of nirvana. The pure *trikāyas* of the Buddha came from this sea of nirvana. The *trikāyas* of the Buddhas are the fields of merit that benefit gods and humans.

Śākyamuni Tathāgata expounded various sutras during his lifetime. The sutras were esoteric or exoteric, Hinayana or Mahayana. Some sutras were canonized by the Kegon, Shingon, and other schools.

[In the *Avataṃsaka-sūtra,*] Vairocana Buddha is established on the lotus flower seat in the center of the worlds of the ten directions. In the *Mahāsaṃnipāta-sūtra,* the Buddhas of the worlds of the ten directions assemble [to hear Śākyamuni Buddha]. In the *Mahāprajñāpāramitā-sūtra,* one thousand Buddhas unanimously expound the teaching that purity and impurity are not different from each other. In the *Mahāvairocana-sūtra* and the *Sarvatathāgatatattvasaṃgraha,* the Buddha reveals himself accompanied by honorable ones numbering one thousand two hundred and more in total.

But in these sutras Śākyamuni Buddha is regarded as having attained enlightenment during his historical life. None of these sutras reveals the originality of Śākyamuni Buddha.

We find in some of these sutras, [as in the *Saddharmapuṇḍarīka-sūtra,*] the statement that one can attain enlightenment in a moment, but there is no mention of the teaching that the seed of Buddhahood was given to living beings by Śākyamuni

Buddha five hundred thousand worlds billion *nayuta asaṃkhya* worlds dust particles *kalpas* ago, and was developed by Mahābhijñājñānābhibhū Buddha three thousand great thousand worlds dust particles *kalpas* ago, and that the Original Śākyamuni Buddha completed [his work of] guiding living beings to perfect enlightenment [when he expounded the *Saddharmapuṇḍarīka-sūtra*.]

The *Avataṃsaka-sūtra* seems to be Perfect Mahayana combined with Specialized Mahayana, and the *Mahāvairocana-sūtra* seems to include the four kinds of teachings, the Hinayana, the Mahayana-cum-Hinayana, the Specialized Mahayana, and the Perfect Mahayana. But when closely examined, both the sutras are Hinayana or Mahayana-cum-Hinayana at most, neither Specialized Mahayana nor Perfect Mahayana, because the two sutras make no mention of the three properties of Buddha-nature[: 1) Buddha-nature in theory, 2) the wisdom that illuminates Buddha-nature, and 3) the ability to perform practices required for developing Buddha-nature into Buddhahood]. How can we obtain the seed of Buddhahood from sutras other than the *Hokekyō*?

[Hsüan-tsang and] other new translators brought Sanskrit texts from India to China and translated them into Chinese. They studied T'ien-t'ai's teaching of one mind–three thousand and appropriated it when they interpreted their canonical sutras. They declared that the teaching of one mind–three thousand was of Indian origin and that they brought it from India. The scholars of the Tendai school today do not know all this and are glad to see that the teachings of the newly introduced sutras and *śāstras* are similar to that of the Tendai school. They treasure texts brought from remote countries and despise those stored in their own libraries. They throw away older texts and cling to new ones. They 275a
are possessed by *māras*. They are foolish indeed.

[No one can attain Buddhahood without the seed of Buddhahood. The seed of Buddhahood is secured only by the teaching of one mind–three thousand. The teaching of one mind–three thousand is expounded only in the *Saddharmapuṇḍarīka-sūtra*.] Attainment of Buddhahood and representing the Most Venerable One in a wooden image or picture will be groundless without the teaching of one mind—three thousand, which secures the seed of Buddhahood.

Question: You have not yet answered my question [as to the existence of the realm of Buddhas in our minds]. Please do [so now].

Answer: It says in the *Muryōgikyō:*

> [Good men or women who hear this sutra]... will be automatically given the merits of the six *pāramitās* even when they are not yet able to perform those *pāramitās*.

Śāriputra addresses the Buddha in the *Hokekyō:*

> [As many gods and dragons as there are sands in the Ganges River... are joining their hands together respectfully,] wishing to hear the Perfect Way.

It says in the *Mahāparinirvāṇa-sūtra,* "*Sa* means 'perfect.'" Nāgārjuna Bodhisattva says, "*Sa* means 'six.'" It says in the *Muemutokudaijōshirongengiki* (*Wu i wu te ta sheng ssu lun hsüan i chi*), "*Sa* is translated as 'six.' The number six means 'perfect' in India." It says in the commentary by Chi-tsang (Kichizō), "*Sa* means 'perfect.'" T'ien-t'ai [Chih-i] Ta-shih says, "*Sa* is a Sanskrit word. It is translated as 'wonderful.'"

I do not like to comment on these statements [because] if I do, I might blaspheme them. However, [I shall try to do so for your sake.

The bodhisattva practices cause the virtues of the Buddha.] The practices and virtues of Śākyamuni, the World-honored One, are contained in the Five Characters: *Myōhō Renge Kyō*. When we keep these Five Characters, we shall automatically receive the merits that the Buddha obtained by his practices.

[In the *Saddharmapuṇḍarīka-sūtra,*] the four great *śrāvakas* [rejoiced at hearing that they were assured of future Buddhahood and] said to the Buddha, "We have automatically obtained an unsurpassed gem although we did not seek one." [When we keep these Five Characters, we shall be automatically endowed with the gem.] This shows that the realm of *śrāvakas* exists in our minds.

The Buddha addresses Śāriputra [in the *Hokekyō*]:

> I once vowed that I would cause all living beings to become exactly as I am. That old vow of mine has now been fulfilled. I lead all living beings into the Way to Buddhahood.

Here we see that Śākyamuni, the World-honored One of Wonderful Enlightenment, is our blood and flesh, and his merits are our bones and marrow.

The Buddha says in the "Chapter on Beholding the Stupa of Treasures" [in the *Hokekyō*]:

> Anyone who protects this sutra should be considered to have already made offerings to Many Treasures [Bodhisattva] and to me...[and] to the Replica-Buddhas who have come here and adorned the worlds with their light.

Here we see that [to protect this sutra, that is, to keep the Five Characters, is to make offerings to] Śākyamuni Buddha, Prabhūtaratna Buddha, and the Replica-Buddhas of the worlds of the ten directions, and therefore that the realm of Buddhas exists in our minds. When we follow them and keep the Five Characters, we shall receive the merits of those Buddhas. Therefore, the Buddha says in the *Saddharmapuṇḍarīka-sūtra,* "If you hear it (the Dharma) even for a moment, you will immediately be able to attain *anuttara-samyak-saṃbodhi."*

The Buddha says in the "Chapter on the Duration of the Life of the Tathāgata"[in the *Hokekyō*]:

> To tell the truth, good men, it has been many hundreds of thousands of billions of *nayuta*s of *kalpa*s since I became the Buddha.

The Buddha who says this is Śākyamuni, the World-honored One, who lives in our minds. "Many hundreds of thousands of billions of *nayuta*s of *kalpa*s" is also expressed as "five hundred thousand billion worlds dust particle *kalpa*s." This is a numerical expression of the Buddha's beginninglessness. [The beginninglessness of the *trikāyas* of Śākyamuni, the World-honored One, is revealed between the lines of this chapter.] The Buddha revealed here is the oldest Buddha without beginning.

The Buddha also says in the same chapter:

> The duration of my life, which I obtained by the practice of the Way of bodhisattvas, has not yet expired. It is twice as long as the length of time previously stated.

This statement means [that the Buddha obtained his eternity by practicing the Way of bodhisattvas and that we are endowed with the ability to practice the Way of bodhisattvas, in other words,] that the realm of bodhisattvas exists in our minds.

[Here we see that the realm of Buddhas and the realm of bodhisattvas are contained in our minds. The same can be said of the other realms.]

The bodhisattvas as numerous as the particles of dust of one thousand worlds who had sprung up from underground are disciples of Śākyamuni, the World-honored One, who lives in our minds. These bodhisattvas are like T'ai-kung (Taikō), Chou-kung-tan (Shūkōtan), and others who were subjects of King Wu (Bu) of the Chou (Shū) dynasty, and who attended the young King Ch'eng-wang (Seiō) [after King Wu's death]; or they are like Take-no-uchi-no-Otodo, who was the first army general under Queen Jingū, and who also served Crown
275b Prince Nintoku. [The four great bodhisattvas among the bodhisattvas who sprang up from underground,] Viśiṣṭacāritra, Anantacāritra, Viśuddhacāritra, and Supratiṣṭhitacāritra, also live in our minds.

Miao-le Ta-shih says:

> Know this! All living beings and their environment are nothing but three thousand things in our minds. When we realize this, we shall be able to attain the fundamental truth that the minds of all living beings pervade the Dharma realm.

During fifty and more years from the time of his enlightenment in the World of Flower Treasury to his *parinirvāṇa* in the Śāla Grove, the Buddha revealed various pure lands. The World

of Flower Treasury was manifested in the *Avataṃsaka-sūtra*. The World of Mystic Adornment was established in the *Mitsugongyō* (*Mi yen ching; Ghanavyūha-sūtra*). The Sāha world was purified and enlarged three times in the *Hokekyō*. The four kinds of Buddha lands were witnessed by the four kinds of people. The one and the same Śāla Grove was seen as the four kinds of Buddha lands by the four kinds of people in the *Zōbōketsugikyō* (*Hsiang fa chüei i ching; Sutra Clearing Doubts Concerning the Semblance Dharma*).

The World of Expedients, the World of Real Rewards, the World of Tranquil Light, the World of Peaceful Nourishment, the World of Pure Lapis Lazuli, and other Buddha lands revealed in these sutras are one or another of the four kinds of Buddha lands. They are subject to change. They are now in the *kalpa* of composition. The Buddhas of these lands are manifestations of the Lord Teacher [Śākyamuni]. Therefore, when the Lord Teacher enters *parinirvāṇa,* they will perish and their worlds also will disappear. However, the Sāha world, of which the Eternal Śākyamuni Buddha is the Lord Teacher, is a permanently existing pure world free from the three calamities and the four *kalpa*s of change. The Buddha has never passed away, nor will he be reborn in the future. The same can be said of the people he teaches. The Buddha as such lives in our minds. Our minds contain three thousand things, including the three phases of existence (i.e., living beings, the five aggregates composing living beings, and their environment).

The eternity of the world of the Eternal Buddha was not expounded in the first fourteen chapters of the *Hokekyō* because the time was not yet ripe for that and also because the hearers had not yet become capable of understanding it. The Five Characters, (when prefixed with *Namu*), *Myōhō Renge Kyō,* are the core of the "Discourse of the Eternal Buddha" in the *Saddharma-puṇḍarīka-sūtra*. The Buddha did not transmit this core even to Mañjuśrī, Bhaiṣajyarāja, or other great bodhisattvas. Needless to say, neither did he do so to the lesser bodhisattvas. The Buddha summoned from underground the bodhisattvas as numerous as the particles of dust of one thousand worlds, expounded to them

the eight chapters (Chapters XV to XXII), and transmitt
core of the sutra to them.

Here is revealed the Most Venerable One in the world.
is a stupa of treasures in the sky above the Sāha world of the
inal Teacher. The stupa of treasures enshrines the *Myōhō*
Kyō. On either side of the *Myōhō Renge Kyō* sit Śākyamuni B
and Prabhūtaratna Buddha. The four bodhisattvas head
Viśiṣṭacāritra accompany Śākyamuni, the World-honored
The four bodhisattvas including Mañjuśrī and Maitreya
lower seats as the attendants of Śākyamuni Buddha. All the
bodhisattvas, major or minor, who are either disciples of th
torical [Buddha] or bodhisattvas who have come from other w
are like nobles and dignitaries who are respected by their su
sitting on the ground. The Buddhas of the worlds of the ten
tions sit on the ground to show that they are emanations of Ś
muni Buddha and that their worlds are reflections of the wo
Śākyamuni Buddha.

The Most Venerable One as such had never been reveale
ing fifty and more years of the Buddha's teaching except i
eight chapters of the *Hokekyō,* which the Buddha expounde
ing his last eight years.

The Age of the Right Teachings of the Buddha and the A
the Counterfeit of the Right Teachings of the Buddha laste
thousand years [after the Buddha's *parinirvāṇa*]. According
Hinayana sutras, Śākyamuni, the World-honored One, was a
panied by Kāśyapa and Ānanda. According to the Provisional M
yana sutras, the *Mahāparinirvāṇa-sūtra,* and the first fourteen
ters of the *Saddharmapuṇḍarīka-sūtra,* Śākyamuni, the W
honored One, was accompanied by Mañjuśrī and Samantabh
The image of the Buddha with this variety of attendants was scu
or painted in those ages, but the image of the Buddha reveal
the "Chapter on the Duration of the Life of the Tathāgata" [i
Saddharmapuṇḍarīka-sūtra] has not yet been created. This i
of the Buddha [accompanied by the four great bodhisattvas
come into existence for the first time in the Age of Degenera

and a half chapters, and the K
plementary to the main part.

The ten volumes including th
be divided into two sections, ea
ductory, main, and supplementa
ductory Chapter" [of the *Saddh*
ductory to the main part. The ei
Expedients" to the "Chapter on
hood of the *Śrāvakas*" are the n
five chapters from the "Chapter
"Chapter on Peaceful Practices"

The Lord Teacher of the first s
enlightenment for the first time i
he expounded the teaching of one
dred realms. This teaching had n
section excels all the sutras ever
yet to be expounded. This sectio
capacity of its hearers into co
expounded in this section is the m
difficult to understand. The hear
seed of Buddhahood by the sixteen
Mahābhijñājñābhibhū Buddha. S
of the seed of Buddhahood within
expounded during the first four [o
teaching, such as the *Avataṃsak*
The Buddha wished to save many.
to save only the few. Those who t
exceptions, just as poison in the b

Adherents of the two vehicle
ually improved their capacity b
during the first four periods of t
realized the existence of the seed o
by hearing the first section of th
Thus they attained enlightenme

The gods and humans who f

of Flower Treasury was manifested in the *Avataṃsaka-sūtra*. The World of Mystic Adornment was established in the *Mitsugongyō* (*Mi yen ching; Ghanavyūha-sūtra*). The Sāha world was purified and enlarged three times in the *Hokekyō*. The four kinds of Buddha lands were witnessed by the four kinds of people. The one and the same Śāla Grove was seen as the four kinds of Buddha lands by the four kinds of people in the *Zōbōketsugikyō* (*Hsiang fa chüei i ching; Sutra Clearing Doubts Concerning the Semblance Dharma*).

The World of Expedients, the World of Real Rewards, the World of Tranquil Light, the World of Peaceful Nourishment, the World of Pure Lapis Lazuli, and other Buddha lands revealed in these sutras are one or another of the four kinds of Buddha lands. They are subject to change. They are now in the *kalpa* of composition. The Buddhas of these lands are manifestations of the Lord Teacher [Śākyamuni]. Therefore, when the Lord Teacher enters *parinirvāṇa,* they will perish and their worlds also will disappear. However, the Sāha world, of which the Eternal Śākyamuni Buddha is the Lord Teacher, is a permanently existing pure world free from the three calamities and the four *kalpa*s of change. The Buddha has never passed away, nor will he be reborn in the future. The same can be said of the people he teaches. The Buddha as such lives in our minds. Our minds contain three thousand things, including the three phases of existence (i.e., living beings, the five aggregates composing living beings, and their environment).

The eternity of the world of the Eternal Buddha was not expounded in the first fourteen chapters of the *Hokekyō* because the time was not yet ripe for that and also because the hearers had not yet become capable of understanding it. The Five Characters, (when prefixed with *Namu*), *Myōhō Renge Kyō,* are the core of the "Discourse of the Eternal Buddha" in the *Saddharma-puṇḍarīka-sūtra*. The Buddha did not transmit this core even to Mañjuśrī, Bhaiṣajyarāja, or other great bodhisattvas. Needless to say, neither did he do so to the lesser bodhisattvas. The Buddha summoned from underground the bodhisattvas as numerous as the particles of dust of one thousand worlds, expounded to them the eight chapters (Chapters XV to XXII), and transmitted the core of the sutra to them.

Here is revealed the Most Venerable One in the world. There is a stupa of treasures in the sky above the Sāha world of the Original Teacher. The stupa of treasures enshrines the *Myōhō Renge Kyō*. On either side of the *Myōhō Renge Kyō* sit Śākyamuni Buddha and Prabhūtaratna Buddha. The four bodhisattvas headed by Viśiṣṭacāritra accompany Śākyamuni, the World-honored One. The four bodhisattvas including Mañjuśrī and Maitreya sit on lower seats as the attendants of Śākyamuni Buddha. All the other bodhisattvas, major or minor, who are either disciples of the Historical [Buddha] or bodhisattvas who have come from other worlds, are like nobles and dignitaries who are respected by their subjects sitting on the ground. The Buddhas of the worlds of the ten directions sit on the ground to show that they are emanations of Śākyamuni Buddha and that their worlds are reflections of the world of Śākyamuni Buddha.

The Most Venerable One as such had never been revealed during fifty and more years of the Buddha's teaching except in the eight chapters of the *Hokekyō,* which the Buddha expounded during his last eight years.

The Age of the Right Teachings of the Buddha and the Age of the Counterfeit of the Right Teachings of the Buddha lasted two thousand years [after the Buddha's *parinirvāṇa*]. According to the Hinayana sutras, Śākyamuni, the World-honored One, was accompanied by Kāśyapa and Ānanda. According to the Provisional Mahayana sutras, the *Mahāparinirvāṇa-sūtra,* and the first fourteen chapters of the *Saddharmapuṇḍarīka-sūtra,* Śākyamuni, the World-honored One, was accompanied by Mañjuśrī and Samantabhadra. The image of the Buddha with this variety of attendants was sculpted or painted in those ages, but the image of the Buddha revealed in the "Chapter on the Duration of the Life of the Tathāgata" [in the *Saddharmapuṇḍarīka-sūtra*] has not yet been created. This image of the Buddha [accompanied by the four great bodhisattvas] will come into existence for the first time in the Age of Degeneration.

Question: You say that the Buddha who is revealed in the "Chapter on the Duration of the Life of the Tathāgata" [in the *Saddharmapuṇḍarīka-sūtra,*] and who is the Most Venerable One accompanied by the four great bodhisattvas, is not yet worshiped by any king or subject in the three countries [of] India, China, and Japan, although temples and stupas have been built in honor of the other Buddhas or Śākyamuni, the World-honored One, as interpreted by the four kinds of reliable bodhisattvas, or by other teachers who studied earlier sutras including the Hinayana sutras and the Provisional Mahayana sutras, and also including the first fourteen chapters of the *Saddharmapuṇḍarīka-sūtra* during the two thousand and more years covering the Age of the Right Teachings of the Buddha and the Age of the Counterfeit of the Right Teachings of the Buddha. I have never heard of this before. I am surprised. I am perplexed. Please say it again. I will listen to you carefully. 275c

Answer: The *Saddharmapuṇḍarīka-sūtra* is composed of eight volumes. It has twenty-eight chapters. Before this sutra, the Buddha expounded many sutras during the first four [of the five] periods of his teaching, and after this sutra he expounded the *Mahāparinirvāṇa-sūtra.* All these sutras can be regarded as a single sutra having [the three parts,] the introductory, main, and supplementary [parts]. The sutras expounded from the time of his enlightenment to the Prajñā[pāramitā] period are introductory to the main part. The ten volumes, including the *Muryōgikyō,* the *Hokekyō,* and the *Kanfugenbosatsugyōbōkyō,* are the main part. The *Mahāparinirvāṇa-sūtra* is supplementary to the main part.

The ten volumes constituting the main part can also be considered to be a single sutra having [the three parts,] introductory, main, and supplementary [parts]. The *Muryōgikyō* and the "Introductory Chapter" of the *Saddharmapuṇḍarīka-sūtra* are introductory to the main part. The fifteen and a half chapters, that is, from the "Chapter on Expedients" to the end of the first nineteen-line verses of the "Chapter on the Variety of Merits," are the main part. The rest of the *Saddharmapuṇḍarīka-sūtra,* which has eleven and a half chapters, and the *Kanfugenbosatsugyōbōkyō* are supplementary to the main part.

The ten volumes including the *Saddharmapuṇḍarīka-sūtra* can be divided into two sections, each having [the three parts,] introductory, main, and supplementary. The *Muryōgikyō* and the "Introductory Chapter" [of the *Saddharmapuṇḍarīka-sūtra*] are introductory to the main part. The eight chapters from the "Chapter on Expedients" to the "Chapter on the Assurance of Future Buddhahood of the *Śrāvaka*s" are the main part of the first section. The five chapters from the "Chapter on the Teacher of Dharma" to the "Chapter on Peaceful Practices" are supplementary.

The Lord Teacher of the first section is the Buddha who attained enlightenment for the first time in his historical life. In this section he expounded the teaching of one thousand suchnesses in one hundred realms. This teaching had never been expounded before. This section excels all the sutras ever expounded, being expounded, and yet to be expounded. This section was taught without taking the capacity of its hearers into consideration. The Right Dharma expounded in this section is the most difficult to believe and the most difficult to understand. The hearers of this section were given the seed of Buddhahood by the sixteenth son of a king, who later became Mahābhijñājñābhibhū Buddha. Some of them realized the existence of the seed of Buddhahood within themselves by hearing the sutras expounded during the first four [of the five] periods of the Buddha's teaching, such as the *Avataṃsaka-sūtra*. But they were very few. The Buddha wished to save many. It was not the Buddha's intention to save only the few. Those who thus attained enlightenment were exceptions, just as poison in the body becomes active unexpectedly.

Adherents of the two vehicles as well as ordinary people gradually improved their capacity by hearing the sutras expounded during the first four periods of the teaching of the Buddha and realized the existence of the seed of Buddhahood within themselves by hearing the first section of the *Saddharmapuṇḍarīka-sūtra*. Thus they attained enlightenment.

The gods and humans who for the first time heard the eight

chapters, consisting of the main part of the first section, directly from the Buddha were various. Some of them obtained the seed of Buddhahood when they heard a phrase or a verse of the main part. Others developed their seed of Buddhahood, while yet others brought the seed of Buddhahood to its fruition. Some attained enlightenment when they heard the *Kanfugenbosatsugyōbōkyō* or the *Mahāparinirvāṇa-sūtra*. Some of those who lived during the Age of the Right Teachings of the Buddha, the Age of the Counterfeit of the Right Teachings of the Buddha, or early in the Age of Degeneration attained the same enlightenment as that which can be attained by hearing the *Saddharmapuṇḍarīka-sūtra* when they heard the Hinayana sutras or the Provisional Mahayana sutras. These people were like those who attained enlightenment when they heard the sutras expounded during the first four [of the five] periods of the teaching of the Buddha.

The second section also has [the three parts,] introductory, main, and supplementary. The first half of the "Chapter on the Appearance of Bodhisattvas from Underground" is introductory; the second half of that chapter, the "Chapter on the Duration of the Life of the Tathāgata," and the first half of the "Chapter on the Variety of Merits" are the main part; the rest is supplementary.

The Lord Teacher of the second section is not Śākyamuni, the World-honored One, who attained enlightenment in his historical life. The teaching of the Buddha is as different from that given in the first section as heaven is different from earth. In the world of the Eternal Śākyamuni Buddha, eternal life is also given not only to the living beings of the ten realms but also to the world itself. Therefore, we can say that the teaching of one mind–three thousand is expounded between the lines of the main part of the second section.

The Buddha says in the first section that the *Hokekyō* excels over all the sutras ever expounded, being expounded, and yet to be expounded. In this statement, the "sutras ever expounded" include the sutras expounded during the first four [of the five] periods of the teaching of the Buddha; the "sutras being expounded"

include the *Muryōgikyō* and the first fourteen chapters of the *Saddharmapuṇḍarīka-sūtra*; and the "sutras yet to be expounded" include the *Mahāparinirvāṇa-sūtra*. But now that the second section has been expounded, we should say that the teachings of the first section are expounded according to the capacity of its hear-
276a ers. The second section is not included in the "sutras being expounded." The second section is the most difficult to believe and the most difficult to understand. It is the teaching expounded without taking the capacity of hearers into consideration.

[Now we have another and the most important teaching of the *Saddharmapuṇḍarīka-sūtra*. As I said previously, the main part of the second fourteen chapters consists of the second half of the "Chapter on the Appearance of Bodhisattvas from Underground," the "Chapter on the Duration of the Life of the Tathāgata," and the first half of the "Chapter on the Variety of Merits." We call this main part the One Chapter and Two Halves. What is expounded in the One Chapter and Two Halves is called the True Dharma.] The True Dharma has its own three parts, the introductory, main, and supplementary [parts].

[The main part of the True Dharma is the One Chapter and Two Halves.] All the other parts of the *Hokekyō* and the other sutras, including the *Saddharmapuṇḍarīka-sūtra* expounded by Mahābhijñājñānābhibhū Buddha in the "Chapter on the Parable of a Magic City," the *Avataṃsaka-sūtra,* the [*Mahā*]*parinirvāṇa-sūtra,* and many other sutras expounded by the Historical Śākyamuni Buddha during the fifty and more years of his life, are introductory to the main part of the True Dharma. The teachings given in this introductory part are Hinayana, wrong teachings, teachings not leading to enlightenment, or teachings not revealing the eternity of the Buddha. Adherents of these teachings are of little virtue and much defilement, ignorant, poor, and lonely. They are like birds and beasts.

The so-called Perfect Mahayana teachings claimed to be included in the sutras expounded before the *Saddharmapuṇḍarīka-sūtra,* or in the first fourteen chapters of the *Saddharmapuṇḍarīka-sūtra,* do not cause people to attain enlightenment. Needless to say, neither do the Hinayana sutras such as the *Mahāvairocana-sūtra* or the teachings of the seven schools such as the Kegon and Shingon schools. We may be able to say that these schools follow the teachings expounded during the first three periods of the Buddha's teaching but, strictly speaking, we should say that they belong to the Hinayana or the Mahayana-cum-Hinayana at most. These schools claim that their teachings are profound but they do not speak of sowing the seed of Buddhahood in the mind of a person, of causing the seed of Buddhahood to develop, or of bringing the seed to fruition. What they call enlightenment is elimination of mind and body like the nirvana without remainder [taught by Hinayana Buddhists]. The seed of Buddhahood is the most important thing for the attainment of Buddhahood. The teachings of these schools say nothing of the sowing, development, and fruition of the seed of Buddhahood. The child of a princess will be worse than a *caṇḍala* if its father is an animal. I will not deal with this matter anymore for now.

The eight chapters constituting the main part of the first fourteen chapters of the *Saddharmapuṇḍarīka-sūtra* seem to have been expounded mainly to adherents of the two vehicles, and additionally to bodhisattvas and ordinary people. But upon close examination, those chapters were expounded mainly to ordinary people [in the three ages after the Buddha's *parinirvāṇa,*] the Age of the Right Teachings of the Buddha, the Age of the Counterfeit of the Right Teachings of the Buddha, and Age of Degeneration. Furthermore, we see that those teachings were expounded especially to those who live at the beginning of the Age of Degeneration.

Question: What does it say in the *Saddharmapuṇḍarīka-sūtra* to prove the truthfulness of your statement?

Answer: The Buddha says in the "Chapter on the Teacher of Dharma," "Many people hate it [this sutra] with jealousy even in my lifetime. Needless to say, more people will do so after my nirvana."

He also says in the "Chapter on Beholding the Stupa of Treasures":

> Those Buddhas employ these expedients in order to preserve the Dharma forever.... The Replica-Buddhas, who have assembled here, wish to know who will do all this.

You also should read the "Chapter on Encouragement of Keeping the Sutra" and the "Chapter on Peaceful Practices." As we see now, even the first fourteen chapters of the *Saddharmapuṇḍarīka-sūtra* include many testimonies to my statement.

When we read the second fourteen chapters of the *Saddharmapuṇḍarīka-sūtra,* we find that the Buddha's discourses in these chapters are given particularly to those who live at the beginning of the Age of Degeneration. According to the verbal expression of the second fourteen chapters, we see that the Buddha attained enlightenment in the remotest past and gave the seed of Buddhahood to his hearers at that time; that the seed of Buddhahood was developed by Mahābhijñājñānābhibhū Buddha and also by Śākyamuni Buddha who expounded the sutras during the first four [of the five] periods of his teaching and the first fourteen chapters of the *Saddharmapuṇḍarīka-sūtra;* and that the seed of Buddhahood finally came to fruition, causing the hearers to reach the stage next to or equivalent to that of the Buddha. But we can see between the lines of the second fourteen chapters that the Buddha speaks directly to those who live at the beginning of the Age of Degeneration throughout the three parts of the section, introductory, main, and supplementary. This is very different from the first fourteen chapters.

The Perfect Mahayana teaching was revealed in the second fourteen chapters of the *Saddharmapuṇḍarīka-sūtra*. The Perfect Mahayana teaching was revived at the beginning of the Age of Degeneration. Therefore, the beginning of the Age of Degeneration is concurrent with the time of the Buddha except for two differences: 1) the seed of Buddhahood was brought to fruition in the lifetime of the Buddha, while the seed of Buddhahood was sown for the first time in the minds of the hearers at the beginning of the Age of Degeneration; and 2) the most important part of the second fourteen chapters was the One Chapter and Two Halves while [the seed of Buddhahood given at the beginning of the Age of Degeneration] is in the form only of the Five Characters, *Myōhō Renge Kyō*.

Question: What does it say in the sutra to prove the truthfulness of your statement?

Answer: It says in the "Chapter on the Appearance of Bodhisattvas from Underground":

> Thereupon the bodhisattva *mahāsattva*s more than eight times the number of the [grains of] sand in the Ganges River, who had come from the other worlds, rose from among the great multitude, joined their hands together toward the Buddha, bowed to him, and said:
>
> "World-honored One! If you permit us to protect, keep, 276b
> read, recite, and copy this sutra, and make offerings to it strenuously in this Sāha world after your extinction, we will do so, and expound it in this world."
>
> Thereupon the Buddha said to those bodhisattva *mahāsattva*s:
>
> "No, good men! I do not want you to protect or keep this sutra...."

This is very different from the five chapters beginning with the "Chapter on the Teacher of Dharma." It says in the "Chapter on Beholding the Stupa of Treasures":

> Thereupon Śākyamuni Buddha...said to the four kinds of devotees with a loud voice:
>
> "Who will expound the *Saddharmapuṇḍarīka-sūtra* in this Sāha world?"
>
> Hearing this, Bhaiṣajyarāja and other great bodhisattvas, as well as Brahmā, Śakra, the Sun God, the Moon God, the

four great heavenly kings, and others, resolved to propagate this sutra. This solicitation was compelling enough to move them because it was made by the Lord Teacher himself. Needless to say, their resolution was strengthened even more when Prabhūtaratna Buddha and the Buddhas of the worlds of the ten directions encouraged them. Hearing their enthusiastic entreaty, the bodhisattvas vowed to propagate this sutra, saying, "We will not spare even our lives." They did so simply to fulfill the request of the Buddha.

But the situation changed greatly after a short time. At the beginning of the "Chapter on the Appearance of Bodhisattvas from Underground," the Buddha refused the proposal of the bodhisattvas numbering more than eight times the number of [grains of] sand in the Ganges River to propagate this sutra in this world. Why was that? It cannot be understood by ordinary people. T'ien t'ai Chih-che Ta-shih says that it was because 1) [they had their own worlds for their mission,] 2) [they had little connection with this world,] and 3) [their activities in this world would block the activities of the bodhisattvas proper to this world]. Therefore, the Buddha summoned his original disciples from underground because 1) [his original disciples would propagate his teaching,] 2) [they were closely connected with this world,] and 3) [they could reveal the eternity of the Buddha]. The Buddha did not transmit the Five Characters, [which he established as] the core of the "Chapter on the Duration of the Life of the Tathāgata," to the great bodhisattvas, who were either disciples of the Historical Buddha or those bodhisattvas who had come from other worlds, because they would not be able to propagate the Five Characters at the beginning of the Age of Degeneration when kings would slander the Dharma and people would be evil. Instead, the Buddha summoned from underground the bodhisattvas as numerous as the particles of dust of one thousand worlds and let them give the Five Characters to the people of Jambudvīpa. He did not give the Five Characters to the disciples of the Historical Buddha because they did not begin to aspire to enlightenment under the guidance of the Original Śākyamuni Buddha, the World-honored One.

T'ien-t'ai [Chih-i] Ta-shih says, "The Buddha says, 'These bodhisattvas are my disciples. They should propagate my teachings.'" Miao-le says, "The teachings of a father, which are propagated by his son, will benefit the whole world." It says in the *Fushōki* (*Fu cheng chi*), "The Dharma realized by the Buddha who attained enlightenment in the remotest past should be transmitted to his disciples who attained enlightenment in the remotest past."

Maitreya Bodhisattva asked a question again, saying:

> We believe that your words given according to the capacities of all living beings are infallible, and that we understand all that you know. But the beginners in bodhisattvahood after your extinction, if they hear these words of yours, will not receive them by faith but commit the sin of violating the Dharma. World-honored One! Explain all this so that we may be able to remove our doubts and so that good people in the future may have no doubts when they hear these words of yours!

This question was made for good people of the future who will have to understand the teaching of the "Chapter on the Duration of the Life of the Tathagāta."

It says in the "Chapter on the Duration of the Life of the Tathāgata":

> Some sons had already lost their right minds while others still had not.... The sons who had not lost their right minds saw that this good medicine had a good color and smell, took it at once, and were cured completely.

This means that all living beings, including bodhisattvas, adher- 276c
ents of the two vehicles, humans, and *deva*s, who received the seed of Buddhahood from Śākyamuni Buddha who had attained enlightenment in the remotest past, and who developed their seed of

Buddhahood by the teachings of Mahābhijñājñānābhibhū Buddha and the first four [of the five] periods of the teaching of the Historical Śākyamuni Buddha, and also by the teachings expounded in the first fourteen chapters of the *Saddharmapuṇḍarīka-sūtra,* finally brought their seed of Buddhahood to fruition when they heard the second fourteen chapters of the sutra.

It goes on to say in the same sutra:

> But the sons who had already lost their right minds did not consent to take the medicine given to them, even though they rejoiced at seeing their father come home and asked him to cure them, because they were so perverted that they did not believe that this medicine having a good color and smell had a good taste.... Now I will have them take it with an expedient.... "I am leaving this good medicine here. Take it! Do not be afraid that you will not be cured!" Having thus advised them, he went to a remote country again. Then he sent home a messenger to tell them....

> It says in the "Chapter on the Variety of Merits," "In the evil world in the age of the decline of my teachings...."

Question: What does it mean to say, "He sent home a messenger to tell them"?

Answer: "A messenger" means the four reliable bodhisattvas. There are four kinds of four reliable bodhisattvas: 1) the four reliable bodhisattvas of the Hinayana sutras, most of whom appeared during the first five hundred years of the Age of the Right Teachings of the Buddha; 2) the four reliable bodhisattvas of the Provisional Mahayana sutras, most of whom appeared in the second five hundred years of the Age of the Right Teachings of the Buddha; 3) the four reliable bodhisattvas of the first fourteen chapters of the *Saddharmapuṇḍarīka-sūtra,* most of whom appeared during the thousand-year Age of the Counterfeit of the Right Teachings of the Buddha, while some appeared at the beginning of the Age of Degeneration; and 4) the four reliable bodhisattvas of the second fourteen chapters of the *Saddharmapuṇḍarīka-sūtra*. The last kind of the four reliable bodhisattvas are the bodhisattvas as numerous as the particles of dust of one thousand worlds who sprang up from underground. They will certainly reappear at the beginning of the Age of Degeneration.

"He sent home a messenger to tell them" means that the Buddha sent the bodhisattvas who had sprung up from underground. "This good medicine" means the *Namu Myōhō Renge Kyō;* that is, the core of the "Chapter on the Duration of the Life of the Tathāgata." The *Namu Myōhō Renge Kyō* is 1) the name of the combination of the Dharma and its simile, 2) the name of the reality of all things, 3) the name of the teaching of the One Vehicle, 4) the name of faith in the Original Buddha, and 5) the name of the supremacy of the teaching. The Buddha did not give this good medicine even to the great disciples of the Historical Buddha. Needless to say, neither did he give it to the bodhisattvas who had come from other worlds.

It says in the "Chapter on the Supernatural Powers of the Tathāgatas":

> Thereupon the bodhisattva *mahāsattva*s as numerous as the particles of dust of one thousand worlds who had sprung up from underground joined their hands together toward the Buddha with all their hearts, looked up at his honorable face, and said to him:
>
> "World-honored One! After your extinction, we will expound this sutra in the worlds of the Replica-Buddhas and also in the place from which you will pass away...."

T'ien-t'ai says, "Only those who had sprung up from underground vowed to propagate this sutra." Tao-hsien says:

> This sutra was transmitted only to the bodhisattvas who had sprung up from underground. Why was that? It was because those bodhisattvas were the disciples of the Buddha who had attained enlightenment in the remotest past. The

> Dharma attained by the oldest Buddha was transmitted to the oldest disciples of the Buddha.

Mañjuśrī Bodhisattva was a disciple of Akṣobhya Buddha of the Golden World in the east. Avalokiteśvara was a disciple of Amitāyus Buddha in the west. Bhaiṣajyarāja Bodhisattva was a disciple of Candrasūryavimalaprabhāsārī Buddha. Samantabhadra Bodhisattva was a disciple of Ratnatejobhyudgatarāja Buddha. They came to the congregation of the *Saddharmapuṇḍarīka-sūtra* to help Śākyamuni, the World-honored One. They were the hearers of the sutras expounded before the *Saddharmapuṇḍarīka-sūtra* or of the first fourteen chapters of the *Saddharmapuṇḍarīka-sūtra*. They were not the keepers of the True Dharma. They were not competent to propagate the True Dharma in the Age of Degeneration.

It says [in the *Saddharmapuṇḍarīka-sūtra*]:

> Thereupon the World-honored One displayed his great supernatural powers in the presence of the multitude.... He stretched out his broad and long tongue upward until the
> 277a tip of it reached the world of Brahmā. The Buddhas who were sitting on the lion seats under the jeweled trees also stretched out their broad and long tongues....

There is no mention of the scene in which Śākyamuni and the other Buddhas sit side by side, and in which the tips of their tongues reach the Heaven of Brahmā, in any other sutra, exoteric or esoteric, Mahayana or Hinayana. It says in the *Sukhāvatīvyūha-sūtra* (*Sutra on Amitāyus*) that the Buddhas [of the worlds of the six directions] stretched out their broad and long tongues to the skies over three thousand worlds, but they did not do so for the purpose of proving the truthfulness of the sutra. It also says in the *Mahāprajñāpāramitā-sūtra* that Śākyamuni Buddha stretched out his broad and long tongue to the skies over three thousand worlds and emitted rays of light before he expounded the *Mahāprajñāpāramitā-sūtra,* but these wonders were not the testimony of the truthfulness of the sutra because these sutras were Perfect Mahayana mixed with Provisional Mahayana, and because they did not reveal the originality of Śākyamuni Buddha.

Śākyamuni Buddha displayed his ten supernatural powers, and transmitted the Five Characters, *Myōhō Renge Kyō,* to the bodhisattvas who had sprung up from underground. It says in the sutra:

> Thereupon the Buddha said to the great bodhisattvas headed by Superior Practice:
>
> "The supernatural powers of the Buddhas are as innumerable, limitless, and inconceivable as previously stated. But I shall not be able to tell all the merits of this sutra to those to whom this sutra is to be transmitted even if I continue telling them by my supernatural powers for many hundreds of thousands of billions of *asaṃkhya*s of *kalpa*s. To sum up, all the teachings of the Tathāgata, all the unhindered, supernatural powers of the Tathāgata, the entire treasury of the hidden core of the Tathāgata, and all the profound achievements of the Tathāgata are revealed and expounded explicitly in this sutra."

T'ien-t'ai says:

> The "Chapter on the Supernatural Powers of the Tathāgatas" consists of three parts: 1)..., 2)..., 3) the summary for transmission. "Thereupon the Buddha said to the great bodhisattvas headed by Superior Practice..." is part three.

Dengyō says:

> The Buddha also says in the "Chapter on the Supernatural Powers of the Tathāgata," "To sum up, all the teachings of the Tathāgata...are revealed and expounded explicitly in this sutra." Here we can say the following definitely. This statement means that all the teachings of the Original Buddha, all the unhindered and supernatural powers of the Original Buddha, the entire treasury of the hidden core of the Original Buddha, and all the profound achievements of

> the Original Buddha are revealed and expounded explicitly in this sutra.

The Buddha gave the Five Characters, *Myōhō Renge Kyō,* to the four great bodhisattvas Viśiṣṭacāritra, Anantacāritra, Viśuddhacāritra, and Supratiṣṭhitacāritra by performing ten wonders. It seems that the first five wonders, [1) stretching out his tongue, 2) emitting rays of light, 3) coughing, 4) snapping, and 5) causing the ground to quake in six ways,] were performed to save people in his lifetime, and that the second five wonders, [1) beholding the great multitude, 2) proclaiming loudly, 3) causing people to worship the Buddha, 4) strewing offerings from afar, and 5) all the worlds turning into a single Buddha land,] were performed for the purpose of leading people after his nirvana. But when we read the sutra carefully, we find that all these ten wonders were performed for the sake of those would live after his nirvana because the Buddha says in the sutra:

> The Buddhas joyfully display their immeasurable supernatural powers because the bodhisattvas from underground vow to keep this sutra after my nirvana.

It says in the "Chapter on Transmission":

> Thereupon Śākyamuni Buddha rose from the seat of the Dharma and by his great supernatural powers put his right hand on the heads of the innumerable bodhisattva *mahāsattvas* and said, "Now I will transmit the Dharma to you...."

Here the Buddha transmitted this sutra to the great multitude, including the bodhisattvas who had sprung up from underground, the bodhisattvas who were the disciples of the Historical Buddha, the bodhisattvas who had come from other worlds, Brahmā, Śakra, the four great heavenly kings, and others. It says in the sutra:

> Thereupon Śākyamuni Buddha, wishing to send back Many Treasures Buddha and the Replica-Buddhas who had come from the worlds of the ten directions to their home worlds,

said, "May the stupa of Many Treasures Buddha be where it was!"

After the Buddha expounded the "Chapter on Transmission," the bodhisattvas from underground retired. In the "Chapter on 277b
the Previous Life of Medicine King Bodhisattva" and in the remaining chapters [of the *Saddharmapuṇḍarīka-sūtra*], and also in [the *Kanfugenbosatsugyōbōkyō* and] the *Mahāparinirvāṇa-sūtra,* the Buddha transmitted this sutra again to the disciples of the Historical Śākyamuni Buddha and to the bodhisattvas who had come from other worlds for the purpose of offering [another] chance to hear this sutra to those who had happened to miss the previous opportunity.

Question: Did the bodhisattvas as numerous as the particles of dust of one thousand worlds who had sprung up from underground appear in Jambudvīpa during the two thousand years from the beginning of the Age of the Right Teachings of the Buddha to the end of the Age of the Counterfeit of the Right Teachings of the Buddha?

Answer: No, they did not.

Question: (With astonishment) The main purpose of the Buddha's expounding the *Saddharmapuṇḍarīka-sūtra,* especially of the second fourteen chapters, was to save those who would live after his nirvana. Therefore, the Buddha transmitted this sutra first to the bodhisattvas as numerous as the particles of dust of one thousand worlds who had sprung up from underground. Why did they not appear and propagate this sutra during the Age of the Right Teachings of the Buddha or during the Age of the Counterfeit of the Right Teachings of the Buddha?

Answer: I do not want to comment on it.

Question: Why not?

Answer: I cannot explain it.

Question: Why not?

Answer: If I do, all the people of the world will have to commit the sin of slandering the Dharma just as the people in the Age of Degeneration did after the nirvana of Powerful Voice King Buddha. Some of my disciples also will slander me if I say anything about the reason they did not. Therefore, I must keep silent.

Question: If you keep silent you will be accused of stinginess.

Answer: What shall I do? I will try to say something about it. In the "Chapter on the Teacher of Dharma," the Buddha says, "Needless to say, more people will do so after my nirvana." He says in the "Chapter on the Duration of the Life of the Tathāgata," "I am leaving this good medicine here." He says in the "Chapter on the Variety of Merits," "[Anyone who keeps this sutra] in the evil world in the age of the decline of my teachings." He says in the "Chapter on the Previous Life of Medicine King Bodhisattva," "Propagate this chapter throughout Jambudvīpa in the latter five hundred years...." He says in the *Mahāparinirvāṇa-sūtra,* "Suppose a couple have seven children. The parents love their children impartially but they love a sick child more deeply than the others."

Judging from the words of the Buddha in these sutras, I can say that the Buddha appeared in this world not for the people [who joined the congregation of the *Saddharmapuṇḍarīka-sūtra* which he expounded] on Mount Gṛdhrakūṭa during the last eight years of his teaching. The Buddha appeared in this world for the people who would live in [the three ages,] the Age of the Right Teachings of the Buddha, the Age of the Counterfeit of the Right Teachings of the Buddha, and the Age of Degeneration. Furthermore, I can say that the Buddha appeared in this world not for the people who lived during two thousand years from the beginning of the Age of the Right Teachings of the Buddha to the end of the Age of the Counterfeit of the Right Teachings of the Buddha but for people like me, who live at the beginning of the Age of Degeneration. "A sick child" means the people who slander the *Saddharmapuṇḍarīka-sūtra* after the

the Buddha's *parinirvāṇa*. "I am leaving this good medicine here" means that the Buddha left this teaching to those who did not believe "that this medicine having a good color and smell had a good taste."

The bodhisattvas as numerous as the particles of dust of one thousand worlds who had sprung up from underground retired and did not reappear during the Age of the Right Teachings of the Buddha and the Age of the Counterfeit of the Right Teachings of the Buddha. The Hinayana teachings and the Provisional Mahayana teachings were to be propagated during the thousand-year Age of the Right Teachings of the Buddha because no one was capable of understanding the Perfect Mahayana teachings. The four kinds of reliable bodhisattvas propagated the Hinayana [and the Provisional Mahayana] during that time. Those who were given the seed of Buddhahood during the lifetime of the Buddha were able to develop their seeds of Buddhahood to fruition through the teachings of the Hinayana or the Provisional Mahayana. Those four kinds of reliable bodhisattvas did not propagate the true teaching [of the *Saddharmapuṇḍarīka-sūtra*] because many of those who were already given the seed of Buddhahood would be perplexed if they had heard a teaching new to them and would become apt to slander the Dharma, delaying their attainment of Buddhahood. The Buddha expounded the Hinayana and the Provisional Mahayana during the first four [of the five] periods of his teaching. The hearers in the first thousand-year age after the Buddha's *parinirvāṇa* were like the hearers in the first four periods of the teaching of the Buddha.

In the middle of the thousand-year Age of the Counterfeit of the Right Teachings of the Buddha, Avalokiteśvara appeared as Nan-yüeh Ta-shih (Nangaku Daishi); and Bhaiṣajyarāja as T'ien-t'ai [Chih-i] Ta-shih. They put more emphasis on the first fourteen chapters than on the second fourteen chapters of the *Saddharmapuṇḍarīka-sūtra* and expounded the teaching of one thousand suchnesses in one hundred realms and the teaching of one mind—three thousand, but they dealt only with contemplating the Dharma, not with practicing the Dharma. To practice the

Dharma means to chant the Five Characters, [*Namu*] *Myōhō Renge Kyō,* before the Most Venerable One revealed in the second fourteen chapters of the *Saddharmapuṇḍarīka-sūtra.* Nan-yüeh and T'ien-t'ai did not deal with this practice because, although some of their hearers were competent enough to understand the Perfect Mahayana teachings, the time was not yet ripe for this practice.

Now we are at the beginning of the Age of Degeneration. We see that the Hinayana Buddhists are beating the Mahayana Buddhists, that the Provisional Mahayana Buddhists are conquering the True Mahayana Buddhists, that some call the east west, and some mistake heaven for earth. Therefore the four kinds of reliable bodhisattvas of the first fourteen chapters of the *Saddharmapuṇḍarīka-sūtra* disappeared and the gods have left
277c this country unprotected. Now the bodhisattvas who are disciples of the Original Buddha should appear from underground and give the good medicine, that is, the Five Characters, *Myōhō Renge Kyō,* to the ignorant people who have not yet been given the seed of Buddhahood. [Those who slander the Dharma will be sent to the evil realms but will benefit from the very sin of slandering the Dharma, just as one who falls to the ground can raise himself up from the same ground.] T'ien-t'ai says, "One who slanders the Dharma will be sent to the evil realms, but will be benefit from the same act of slandering the Dharma."

My disciples! Think this over. The bodhisattvas as numerous as the particles of dust of one thousand worlds who had sprung up from underground aspired to enlightenment for the first time under the guidance of the Lord Teacher Śākyamuni, the World-honored One. They did not appear in this world when Śākyamuni Buddha attained enlightenment in his historical life or when he entered *parinirvāṇa* at the Śāla Grove. They should be accused of unfiliality. They did not come to this world when the Buddha expounded the first fourteen chapters of the *Saddharmapuṇḍarīka-sūtra* either. They were absent from the last six chapters of the sutra. They were present only in the eight chapters (from Chapters XV to XXII). They were exceptionally great bodhisattvas. Such great bodhisattvas received the Five Characters and vowed to propagate this sutra in the Age of Degeneration. They vowed this in the presence of Śākyamuni, Prabhūtaratna, and the Buddhas of the worlds of the ten directions. How can it be that they will not reappear at the beginning of the Age of Degeneration?

Know this! When the four great bodhisattvas vigorously propagate the Dharma, they will appear as wise kings and criticize unwise kings; when they are passive they will appear as priests and keep the Right Dharma.

Question: What did the Buddha say about this?

Answer: The Buddha says, "Propagate this chapter throughout Jambudvīpa in the latter five hundred years after my extinction." T'ien-t'ai [Chih-i] Ta-shih says, "The Wonderful Way will benefit people who will live as late as during the last five hundred years." Miao-le comments on this, saying, "We cannot say that there will be no benefit at the beginning of the Age of Degeneration." Dengyō Daishi says:

> The Age of the Right Teachings of the Buddha is already past. The Age of the Counterfeit of the Right Teachings of the Buddha is now ending. The Age of Degeneration is near at hand.

"The Age of Degeneration is near at hand" means that the time of Dengyō Daishi was not yet the right time to propagate the Wonderful Way. Dengyō Daishi of Japan predicted the condition of the beginning of the Age of Degeneration, saying:

> After the end of the Age of the Counterfeit of the Right Teachings of the Buddha, the Age of Degeneration will begin in a country east of T'ang and west of Chieh. The people of this country will be of the five defilements. They will be in conflict with each other. The Buddha says in the *Saddharmapuṇḍarīka-sūtra,* "Many people hate [this sutra] with jealousy even in my lifetime. Needless to say, more people will do so after my nirvana." What he says is true.

"They will be in conflict with each other" predicts the two calamities: civil wars and [foreign] invasions from the western sea.

In this Age of Degeneration, the bodhisattvas as numerous as the particles of dust of one thousand worlds will spring up again from underground to this country and accompany the Most Venerable One who revealed himself in the second fourteen chapters of the *Saddharmapuṇḍarīka-sūtra*. The Most Venerable One in Jambudvīpa will be established in this country.

This Most Venerable One has never been established in India or China. Jōgū Taishi had Shitennōji built but enshrined there Amitābha Buddha, the Buddha of a world outside the Sāha world, because the time was not yet ripe [for enshrining the Buddha of the *Saddharmapuṇḍarīka-sūtra*]. Emperor Shōmu had Tōdaiji built and enshrined the Lord Teacher of the *Avataṃsaka-sūtra* there. The true teaching of the *Saddharmapuṇḍarīka-sūtra* had not yet been revealed by him. Dengyō Daishi propagated the true teaching of the *Saddharmapuṇḍarīka-sūtra* but did so imperfectly. He had Kompon-chūdō built on Mount Hiei but enshrined Bhaiṣajyaguru Tathāgata of the eastern world there, not [Śākyamuni Buddha accompanied by] the four bodhisattvas who were the leading disciples of the Original Śākyamuni Buddha, because he knew it should be [in the Age of Degeneration] that Śākyamuni Buddha, accompanied by the bodhisattvas as numerous as the particles of dust of one thousand worlds who had sprung up from underground [as described in the *Saddharmapuṇḍarīka-sūtra*], be enshrined as the Most Venerable One.

These bodhisattvas who received the order from the Buddha are now staying underground. They did not appear in this world in the Age of the Right Teachings of the Buddha or in the Age of the Counterfeit of the Right Teachings of the Buddha. If they do not appear in the Age of Degeneration, they will be great liars. Their vow to Śākyamuni, Prabhūtaratna, and the Buddhas of the worlds of the ten directions will be broken.

Now we have had great earthquakes, appearances of comets, and other calamities in recent years. These calamities were not seen

in the Age of the Right Teachings of the Buddha or in the Age of the Counterfeit of the Right Teachings of the Buddha. These calamities were not caused by *garuḍas*, *asuras*, or dragons. They must be 278a
an omen that the four great bodhisattvas will appear [in this country]. T'ien-t'ai says, "When a rainfall is heavy, we know that the dragon [that causes the rainfall] is large. When we see beautiful lotus flowers, we know that the pond is deep." Miao-le says, "A wise man knows why an incident happens. A snake knows snakes."

When the sun shines brightly, everything is visible on the earth. One who knows the *Hokekyō* will be able to realize what caused the recent calamities. Out of his compassion toward the ignorant people who live in the Age of Degeneration, and who do not know the gem of the teaching of one mind–three thousand, the Buddha puts this gem into the bag of the Five Characters and hangs this bag around their necks. The four great bodhisattvas will protect them just as T'ai-kung and Chou-kung guarded King Ch'eng-wang or the Four Elders served Emperor Hui-ti (Keitei).

Written on the twenty-fifth day of the fourth month of the tenth year of Bun-ei by Nichiren.

Glossary

Age of Conflicts: The period following the Age of Degeneration, when the Buddha's teaching is no longer present in the world. *See also* Age of Degeneration; five periods of teaching.

Age of Degeneration: The period of a thousand years following the Age of the Counterfeit of the Right Teachings of the Buddha, in which only the teaching of the Buddha exists but correct practice is no longer possible. *See also* Age of the Counterfeit of the Right Teachings of the Buddha; five periods of teaching.

Age of the Counterfeit of the Right Teachings of the Buddha: The period of a thousand years following the Age of the Right Teachings of the Buddha, in which the Buddha's teaching is practiced but enlightenment is no longer possible. *See also* Age of the Right Teachings of the Buddha; five periods of teaching.

Age of the Right Teachings of the Buddha: The period of five hundred years after Śākyamuni Buddha's *parinirvāṇa,* in which his teaching is properly practiced and enlightenment can be attained. *See also* five periods of teaching.

arhat ("worthy one"): A saint who has completely eradicated evil passions and attained liberation from the cycle of birth and death (samsara); arhatship is the highest of the four stages of spiritual attainment in the Hinayana. *See also* Hinayana.

asura: A class of demonic beings who are in constant conflict with the gods.

Avīci Hell: The lowest of the various levels of hells in Buddhist cosmology; also called the Hell of Incessant Suffering; those who have committed the five grave offenses and slandered the Dharma are consigned to this hell. *See also* five grave offenses.

birth and death: The cycle of birth and death (samsara) through which beings transmigrate due to karmic causes; the world of suffering, contrasted with the bliss of nirvana. *See also* nirvana.

bodhi: Enlightenment; the state of the highest perfection of wisdom in which one is awakened to the true nature of things.

bodhisattva ("enlightenment being"): In the Mahayana, one who has made vows to save suffering beings and attain enlightenment through the practice of the *pāramitās*, which leads ultimately to Buddhahood. Bodhisattvas vow to refrain from entering nirvana until all sentient beings are liberated. *See also* Buddhahood; Mahayana; nirvana; *pāramitās*.

Brahmanism: The religious and philosophical teachings of ancient India that formed the basis of Hinduism; its primary texts are the four Vedas.

Buddhahood: The state of becoming a Buddha; the goal of the bodhisattva path.

Buddha land: A world or realm in which a particular Buddha dwells. *See also* Pure Land.

Buddha-nature: The basic enlightened nature of sentient beings, which is chronically obscured by their ignorance. The complete unfolding of Buddha-nature is enlightenment.

caṇḍāla: An outcaste; a member of the lowest social class in Indian society.

Confucianism: An ethical, religious system of China originating in the teaching of Confucius, centering around filial duty and emphasizing the virtues of benevolence and propriety.

enlightenment. *See bodhi.*

five aggregates (*skandhas*): The five constituent elements of sentient beings—1) form (*rūpa*), 2) sensation (*vedanā*), 3) conception (*saṃjñā*), 4) volition (*saṃskāra*), and 5) consciousness (*vijñāna*).

five grave offenses: The five most serious offenses, commission of which relegates one to the Avīci Hell—1) patricide, 2) matricide, 3) killing an arhat, 4) maliciously harming a Buddha, and 5) causing discord in the Buddhist order (sangha). *See also* arhat; Avīci Hell.

five periods of teaching: The five five hundred-year periods of the Buddha's teaching predicted to occur after Śākyamuni's *parinirvāṇa:* 1) in the first period, Buddhist practitioners are able to attain enlightenment and liberation, 2) in the second, they steadfastly practice meditation, 3) in the third, they eagerly listen to Buddhist teachings, 4) in the fourth, their practice consists of building temples and stupas, and 5) in the fifth, they engage in doctrinal disputes. These periods represent the gradual decline of Buddhist practice and correspond to the Age of the Right Teachings of the Buddha (1), the Age of the Counterfeit of the Right Teachings of the Buddha (2–3), and the Age of Degeneration (4–5). After these three ages comes the Age of Conflicts, in which the Buddhist teachings are no longer present in the world. *See also* Age of Conflicts; Age of Degeneration; Age of the Counterfeit of the Right Teachings of the Buddha; Age of the Right Teachings of the Buddha; Śākyamuni.

four continents: The four large land masses that surround Mount Sumeru, each in one of the cardinal directions. Jambudvīpa, in the south, corresponds to the Indian subcontinent. *See also* Jambudvīpa; Mount Sumeru.

four kinds of devotees: The four groups of Buddhist followers—monks (*bhikṣus*), nuns (*bhikṣuṇīs*), laymen (*upāsakas*), and laywomen (*upasīkās*).

garuḍa: A mythological giant bird.

gāthā: A verse of Buddhist scripture or teachings; a Buddhist hymn.

Hinayana ("Lesser Vehicle"): A derogatory term applied by Mahayana Buddhists to various early schools of Buddhism whose primary soteriological aim is individual salvation. There are four stages of spiritual attainment in the Hinayana: stream-winner, once-returner, non-returner, and arhat. The paths of the *śrāvaka* and *pratyekabuddha,* collectively known as the two vehicles, are part of the Hinayana path to arhatship. *See also* arhat; Mahayana; non-returner; once-returner; *pratyekabuddha; śrāvaka;* stream-winner; two vehicles.

icchantika: One who has no stock of good merit and thus no possibility of attaining Buddhahood.

Jambudvīpa: In Buddhist cosmology, the triangular continent situated to the south of Mount Sumeru, corresponding to the Indian subcontinent; one of the four continents inhabited by human beings. *See also* four continents; Mount Sumeru.

kalpa: An immense period of time, an eon; an *asaṃkhya kalpa* is an "incalculable" eon.

kṣatriya: A warrior or noble; a member of the ruling class in Indian society.

Lotus Sutra: The popular, abbreviated name for the *Saddharmapuṇḍarīka-sūtra* (*Scripture of the Lotus Blossom of the Fine Dharma*), one of the most important Mahayana sutras in East Asian Buddhism, which presents the teaching of the One Vehicle. Nichiren extolled the virtues of practicing this sutra (Japanese, *Hokekyō*) above all other practices and scriptural teachings. The primary practice of the Nichiren school of Japanese Buddhism, established on the basis of the *Lotus Sutra,* is recitation of the name of the sutra: *(Namu) Myōhō Renge Kyō. See also* Mahayana; *Myōhō Renge Kyō;* One Vehicle.

mahāsattva ("great being"): Synonym for a bodhisattva. *See* bodhisattva.

Mahayana ("Great Vehicle"): One of the two major schools of Buddhism, along with the Hinayana. The spiritual ideal of the the Mahayana is the bodhisattva, who vows to bring all sentient beings to Buddhahood. *See also* bodhisattva; Hinayana.

māra: A kind of demon that hinders Buddhist practice.

Middle Way: The truth of nonduality taught by Śākyamuni Buddha.

Most Venerable One: According to Nichiren in the *Kanjinhonzonshō,* the Most Venerable One is Śākyamuni Buddha as he appears in the stupa of the Buddha Prabhutaratna in the "Chapter on Beholding the Stupa of Treasures" in the *Lotus Sutra. See also Lotus Sutra;* Śākyamuni.

Mount Gṛdhrakūṭa ("Vulture Peak"): A mountain in northeast India where the Buddha was said to have delivered many important sutras, including the *Lotus Sutra. See also Lotus Sutra.*

Mount Hiei: Along with Nara, one of the two principal centers of traditional Buddhist learning in Japan; the monastic center of the Tendai school. Many Buddhist teachers of the Kamakura period (1185–1332), including Nichiren, originally studied there. *See also* Nara.

Mount Sumeru: In Buddhist cosmology, the highest mountain rising from the center of the world; it is surrounded by the four continents inhabited by human beings, including Jambudvīpa. *See also* four continents; Jambudvīpa.

Myōhō Renge Kyō: The name of the *Lotus Sutra;* in the *Kanjinhonzonshō,* Nichiren holds that this mantra, also called the Five Characters, represents not only the name of the *Lotus Sutra* but the Dharma taught in the sutra. *See also Lotus Sutra.*

Nara: Along with Mount Hiei, one of the two principal centers of traditional Buddhist learning in Japan; headquarters of several schools of Japanese Buddhism. *See also* Mount Hiei.

nirvana: Liberation from the cycle of birth and death, a state in which all evil passions are extinguished and the highest wisdom attained; *bodhi,* enlightenment. *See also* birth and death; *bodhi.*

non-returner (*anāgāmin*): The third of the four stages of spiritual attainment in the Hinayana; one who has attained this stage is no longer subject to rebirth in the world of desire in the triple world. *See also* Hinayana; triple world.

once-returner (*sakṛdāgāmin*): The second of the four stages of spiritual attainment in the Hinayana; one who has attained this state is subject to rebirth only once in each of the human and the heavenly realms of the triple world before attaining nirvana. *See also* Hinayana; nirvana; triple world.

One Vehicle: The teaching of the *Lotus Sutra* that all beings are destined for the single goal of Buddhahood, and that the path of the bodhisattva, the Mahayana, or Great Vehicle, is the way to enlightenment. The One Vehicle teaching is contrasted to and elevated above the teaching of the two vehicles, i.e., the paths of the *śrāvaka*s and the *pratyekabuddha*s. *See also Lotus Sutra;* Mahayana; *śrāvaka; pratyekabuddha;* two vehicles.

*pāramitā*s: Six practices to be perfected by bodhisattvas on the path to Buddhahood—1) generosity (*dāna*), 2) observance of the precepts (*śīla*), 3) patience (*kṣānti*), 4) effort (*vīrya*), 5) meditation (*dhyāna*), and 6) wisdom (*prajñā*).

parinirvāṇa: Complete nirvana, commonly used to describe the nirvana of the Buddha. *See also* nirvana.

pratyekabuddha ("solitary enlightened one"): One who has attained enlightenment directly, without the guidance of a teacher, and who does not teach others; along with the path of the *śrāvaka*, one of the two vehicles of the Hinayana. *See also* Hinayana; *śrāvaka;* two vehicles.

precepts: Vows concerning moral conduct taken by lay Buddhists and monastics. The five basic precepts to be followed by all Buddhists are: 1) not to kill; 2) not to steal; 3) not to engage in sexual conduct, for monastics, or commit adultery, for lay Buddhists; 4) not to use false speech; and 5) not to ingest intoxicants.

Pure Land: Generally, any Buddha land; specifically, refers to the Buddha land in the West inhabited by Amitābha Buddha, rebirth in which is the focus of the Pure Land (Jōdo) school.

rākṣasī: A female flesh-eating demon (*rākṣasa*).

Replica-Buddhas: Different manifestations of a Buddha; the Buddha can manifest an infinite number of times and appear in innumerable worlds simultaneously in order to help sentient beings. In the *Lotus Sutra* Śākyamuni summons his Replica-Buddhas from throughout the universe. *See also* Śākyamuni; *Lotus Sutra.*

Saddharmapuṇḍarīka-sūtra. See Lotus Sutra.

Sāha ("Endurance") world: The world of human beings' existence; this world of suffering.

Śākyamuni: The Historical Buddha, born Prince Siddhārtha to a royal family in northern India in the fifth century B.C.E. As a young man he left his privileged life to seek the truth and became the Buddha (Awakened One) upon his attainment of enlightenment; he traveled throughout northern India teaching the Dharma, until passing into *parinirvāṇa* at the age of eighty. His life and teachings form the basis for Buddhism. In these texts, Nichiren also refers to Śākyamuni as the Original Buddha and the Original Teacher.

samādhi: A mental state of concentration involving the focusing of thought on one object. Also called meditation.

samsara. *See* birth and death.

śāstra: A Buddhist treatise, a scholastic work, or a commentary on a sutra.

six realms: The six samsaric states of existence into which beings may be born: the realm of hell, the realm of hungry ghosts (*preta*s), the realm of animals, the realm of humans, the realm of *asura*s, and the realm of gods (*deva*s).

śrāmaṇa: A renunciant, another name for a Buddhist monk, originally applied to those who practiced asceticism.

śrāvaka ("word-hearer"): Originally, a disciple of the Buddha, one of those who heard him expound the teachings directly; generally, one who seeks to attain individual nirvana; along with the path of the *pratyekabuddha*, one of the two vehicles of the Hinayana. *See also* Hinayana; *pratyekabuddha;* two vehicles.

stream-winner (*srota-āpanna*): The first of the four stages of spiritual attainment in the Hinayana; one who has entered the stream of the Dharma by destroying various wrong views. *See also* Hinayana.

stupa: A reliquary, a roughly hemispherical structure enshrining the relics of the Buddha or some other Buddhist teacher, or copies of Buddhist scriptures.

suchness (*tathatā*): The state of things as they really are; the ultimate truth; ultimate reality.

sutra: A discourse of the Buddha.

Taoism: An indigenous Chinese religious philosophy, based on belief in the invisible, underlying principle of the universe called the *tao* ("way") and the balance of positive and negative energies (*yin* and *yang*). Taoism became a dominant religion that coexisted with the Confucian sociopolitical structure of Chinese society.

Tathāgata ("one who has come from suchness"): An epithet for a Buddha. *See also* suchness.

tathāgatagarbha ("womb of suchness"): Another name for the Buddha-nature that is within all beings, conceived of as a kind of womblike storehouse or receptacle where the seed of Buddhahood is retained and matured. *See also* Buddhahood; Buddha-nature.

*trikāya*s: The three bodies in which a Buddha may take form: the Dharma body (*dharmakāya*), the primordial body of a Buddha, which is identical with true suchness, nirvana; the enjoyment body (*saṃbhogakāya*), acquired by Buddhas upon the absolute perfection of their practice; and the transformation body (*nirmāṇakāya*), an infinite number of forms in which Buddhas, out of their great compassion, reveal themselves to help sentient beings. *See also* nirvana; suchness.

Tripiṭaka: The three "baskets" (*piṭaka*s) or categories of the early Buddhist (Hinayana) teachings—1) the sutras, discourses of the Buddha; 2) the Vinaya, monastic rules of conduct; and 3) the Abhidharma, commentaries on the Buddha's teachings.

triple world: The three classifications of samsaric states of existence: the world of desire (*kāmadhātu*), this world of suffering; the world of form (*rūpadhātu*) inhabited by those who have severed all desires but still experience the world as form; and the world of non-form (*ārūpyadhātu*), inhabited by those who have severed all desires and attachment to form but have not yet attained enlightenment.

two vehicles: The teachings and paths of practice for *śrāvaka*s and *pratyekabuddhas*. *See also pratyekabuddha; śrāvaka.*

wheel-turning holy king (*cakravartin*): The ideal king or universal monarch, as conceived of in Indian philosophy, who rules the world with a special wheel (*cakra*) that flies through the air and destroys his enemies.

zazen: The practice of sitting meditation; the primary practice of the Zen (Chinese: Ch'an) school of Mahayana Buddhism.

Bibliography

Murano, Senchū, trans. *Risshō-ankoku-ron, or, Establish the Right Law and Save Our Country*. Tokyo: Nichiren Shū Headquarters, 1977.

Renondeau, C., trans. *La doctrine de Nichiren*. Paris: Presses Universitaires de France, 1953.

Seikyo Times, trans. *The Major Writings of Nichiren Daishonin*. Tokyo: Nichiren Shoshu International Center, 1979–90.

Tanabe, George, Jr., ed. *Writings of Nichiren Shōnin: Doctrine 2*. Compiled by Kyōtsū Hori. Tokyo: Nichiren Shū Overseas Propagation Promotion Association, 2002.

Yampolsky, Philip B., ed. *Letters of Nichiren*. Translated by Burton Watson, et al. New York: Columbia University Press, 1996.

—. *Selected Writings of Nichiren*. Translated by Burton Watson, et al. New York: Columbia University Press, 1996.

Index

A

Adamantine Pinnacle Sutra. See Sarvatathāgatatattvasaṃgraha
Āgama sutras 77
Age of Conflicts 58
Age of Degeneration 21, 27, 58, 73, 74, 78, 92, 95, 97, 98–9, 100, 102, 103, 104, 108, 109, 110, 111, 112, 113
Age of the Counterfeit of the Right Teachings of the Buddha 21, 58, 73, 78, 92, 93, 95, 97, 102, 107, 108, 109, 111, 112, 113
Age of the Right Teachings of the Buddha 21, 58, 73, 78, 92, 93, 95, 97, 102, 107, 108, 109, 111, 112, 113
Ākāśgarbha 28
Akṣobhya 41, 104
alms 38, 42
almsgivers, almsgiving 17, 19, 20, 21, 49
Amitābha 6, 11, 24, 25, 26, 27, 28, 31, 32, 33, 34, 43, 112
Amitāyurdhyāna-sūtra. See Kammuryōjukyō
Amitāyus 104
Amoghavajra 85
anāgāmin. See non-returner
Ānanda 75, 92
Anantacāritra 55, 90, 106
anuttara-samyak-saṃbodhi (*see also* enlightenment, perfect) 70, 89
arhat(s) (*see also* saint) 16, 20, 39
arhatship 21, 71, 79
Asia 6
asuras 69, 70, 73, 113
Aśvaghoṣa 80, 82
Avalokiteśvara 28, 79, 104, 109
Avataṃsaka period 75
Avataṃsaka-sūtra 75, 77, 78, 81, 86, 87, 91, 94, 96, 112
Avīci Hell (*see also* Hell of Incessant Suffering) 27, 39, 42, 45, 49, 50, 51
Awa 5

B

Balin Asura King 70
Bamboo Stick 45
Bhaiṣajyaguru 11, 28, 112
Bhaiṣajyaguruvaiḍūryaprabhāsa-pūrvapraṇidhānaviśeṣavistara. See Yakushikyō
Bhaiṣajyarāja 55, 91, 99, 104, 109
bhikṣu(s) (*see also* monk) 38, 70, 72
bhikṣuṇī(s) (*see also* nun) 38, 70, 72
birth and death 13, 26, 31, 80
Bodh Gayā 55
bodhi (*see also* enlightenment) 41
bodhisattva(s) 20, 24, 27, 28, 32, 37, 39, 47, 55, 68, 69, 70, 75, 76,

P

R

U

V

W

Y

Z

A List of the Volumes of the BDK English Tripiṭaka (First Series)

Abbreviations

Ch.:	Chinese
Skt.:	Sanskrit
Jp.:	Japanese
Eng.:	Published title
T.:	Taishō Tripiṭaka

Vol. No.		Title	*T.* No.
1, 2	*Ch.*	Ch'ang-a-han-ching (長阿含經)	1
	Skt.	Dīrghāgama	
3–8	*Ch.*	Chung-a-han-ching (中阿含經)	26
	Skt.	Madhyamāgama	
9-I	*Ch.*	Ta-ch'eng-pên-shêng-hsin-ti-kuan-ching (大乘本生心地觀經)	159
9-II	*Ch.*	Fo-so-hsing-tsan (佛所行讃)	192
	Skt.	Buddhacarita	
10-I	*Ch.*	Tsa-pao-ts'ang-ching (雜寶藏經)	203
	Eng.	The Storehouse of Sundry Valuables	
10-II	*Ch.*	Fa-chü-p'i-yü-ching (法句譬喩經)	211
	Eng.	The Scriptural Text: Verses of the Doctrine, with Parables	
11-I	*Ch.*	Hsiao-p'in-pan-jo-po-lo-mi-ching (小品般若波羅蜜經)	227
	Skt.	Aṣṭasāhasrikā-prajñāpāramitā-sūtra	
11-II	*Ch.*	Chin-kang-pan-jo-po-lo-mi-ching (金剛般若波羅蜜經)	235
	Skt.	Vajracchedikā-prajñāpāramitā-sūtra	

Vol. No.		Title	*T.* No.
11-III	*Ch.*	Jên-wang-pan-jo-po-lo-mi-ching (仁王般若波羅蜜經)	245
	Skt.	Kāruṇikārājā-prajñāpāramitā-sūtra (?)	
11-IV	*Ch.*	Pan-jo-po-lo-mi-to-hsing-ching (般若波羅蜜多心經)	251
	Skt.	Prajñāpāramitāhṛdaya-sūtra	
12-I	*Ch.*	Ta-lo-chin-kang-pu-k'ung-chên-shih-san-mo-yeh-ching (大樂金剛不空眞實三麼耶經)	243
	Skt.	Adhyardhaśatikā-prajñāpāramitā-sūtra	
12-II	*Ch.*	Wu-liang-shou-ching (無量壽經)	360
	Skt.	Sukhāvatīvyūha	
	Eng.	The Larger Sutra on Amitāyus (In The Three Pure Land Sutras)	
12-III	*Ch.*	Kuan-wu-liang-shou-fo-ching (觀無量壽佛經)	365
	Skt.	Amitāyurdhyāna-sūtra	
	Eng.	The Sutra on Contemplation of Amitāyus (In The Three Pure Land Sutras)	
12-IV	*Ch.*	A-mi-t'o-ching (阿彌陀經)	366
	Skt.	Sukhāvatīvyūha	
	Eng.	The Smaller Sutra on Amitāyus (In The Three Pure Land Sutras)	
12-V	*Ch.*	Ti-ts'ang-p'u-sa-pên-yüan-ching (地藏菩薩本願經)	412
	Skt.	Kṣitigarbhapraṇidhāna-sūtra (?)	
12-VI	*Ch.*	Yao-shih-liu-li-kuang-ju-lai-pên-yüan-kung-tê-ching (藥師琉璃光如來本願功德經)	450
	Skt.	Bhaiṣajyaguruvaiḍūryaprabhāsapūrva-praṇidhānaviśeṣavistara	
12-VII	*Ch.*	Mi-lê-hsia-shêng-ch'êng-fo-ching (彌勒下生成佛經)	454
	Skt.	Maitreyavyākaraṇa (?)	
12-VIII	*Ch.*	Wên-shu-shih-li-wên-ching (文殊師利問經)	468
	Skt.	Mañjuśrīparipṛcchā (?)	
13-I	*Ch.*	Miao-fa-lien-hua-ching (妙法蓮華經)	262
	Skt.	Saddharmapuṇḍarīka-sūtra	
	Eng.	The Lotus Sutra	
13-II	*Ch.*	Wu-liang-i-ching (無量義經)	276

Vol. No.		Title	*T.* No.
13-III	*Ch.*	Kuan-p‘u-hsien-p‘u-sa-hsing-fa-ching (觀普賢菩薩行法經)	277
14–19	*Ch.*	Ta-fang-kuang-fo-hua-yen-ching (大方廣佛華嚴經)	278
	Skt.	Avataṃsaka-sūtra	
20-I	*Ch.*	Shêng-man-shih-tzŭ-hou-i-ch‘eng-ta-fang-pien-fang-kuang-ching (勝鬘師子吼一乘大方便方廣經)	353
	Skt.	Śrīmālādevīsiṃhanāda-sūtra	
20-II	*Ch.*	Chin-kuang-ming-tsui-shêng-wang-ching (金光明最勝王經)	665
	Skt.	Suvarṇaprabhāsa-sūtra	
21–24	*Ch.*	Ta-pan-nieh-p‘an-ching (大般涅槃經)	374
	Skt.	Mahāparinirvāṇa-sūtra	
25-I	*Ch.*	Fo-ch‘ui-pan-nieh-p‘an-liao-shuo-chiao-chieh-ching (佛垂般涅槃略説教誡經)	389
25-II	*Ch.*	Pan-chou-san-mei-ching (般舟三昧經)	418
	Skt.	Pratyutpannabuddhasammukhāvasthitasamādhi-sūtra	
	Eng.	The Pratyutpanna Samādhi Sutra	
25-III	*Ch.*	Shou-lêng-yen-san-mei-ching (首楞嚴三昧經)	642
	Skt.	Śūraṅgamasamādhi-sūtra	
	Eng.	The Śūraṅgama Samādhi Sutra	
25-IV	*Ch.*	Chieh-shên-mi-ching (解深密經)	676
	Skt.	Saṃdhinirmocana-sūtra	
	Eng.	The Scripture on the Explication of Underlying Meaning	
25-V	*Ch.*	Yü-lan-p‘ên-ching (盂蘭盆經)	685
	Skt.	Ullambana-sūtra (?)	
25-VI	*Ch.*	Ssŭ-shih-êrh-chang-ching (四十二章經)	784
26-I	*Ch.*	Wei-mo-chieh-so-shuo-ching (維摩詰所説經)	475
	Skt.	Vimalakīrtinirdeśa-sūtra	
26-II	*Ch.*	Yüeh-shang-nü-ching (月上女經)	480
	Skt.	Candrottarādārikāparipṛcchā	

Vol. No.		Title	T. No.
26-III	*Ch.*	Tso-ch'an-san-mei-ching (坐禪三昧經)	614
26-IV	*Ch.*	Ta-mo-to-lo-ch'an-ching (達磨多羅禪經)	618
	Skt.	Yogācārabhūmi-sūtra (?)	
27	*Ch.*	Yüeh-têng-san-mei-ching (月燈三昧經)	639
	Skt.	Samādhirājacandrapradīpa-sūtra	
28	*Ch.*	Ju-lêng-ch'ieh-ching (入楞伽經)	671
	Skt.	Laṅkāvatāra-sūtra	
29-I	*Ch.*	Ta-fang-kuang-yüan-chio-hsiu-to-lo-liao-i-ching (大方廣圓覺修多羅了義經)	842
29-II	*Ch.*	Su-hsi-ti-chieh-lo-ching (蘇悉地羯囉經)	893
	Skt.	Susiddhikaramahātantrasādhanopāyika-paṭala	
	Eng.	The Susiddhikara Sutra (In Two Esoteric Sutras)	
29-III	*Ch.*	Mo-têng-ch'ieh-ching (摩登伽經)	1300
	Skt.	Mātaṅgī-sūtra (?)	
30-I	*Ch.*	Ta-p'i-lu-chê-na-chêng-fo-shên-pien-chia-ch'ih-ching (大毘盧遮那成佛神變加持經)	848
	Skt.	Mahāvairocanābhisambodhivikurvitādhiṣṭhāna-vaipulyasūtrendrarāja-nāma-dharmaparyāya	
30-II	*Ch.*	Ching-kang-ting-i-ch'ieh-ju-lai-chên-shih-shê-ta-ch'eng-hsien-chêng-ta-chiao-wang-ching (金剛頂一切如來眞實攝大乘現證大教王經)	865
	Skt.	Sarvatathāgatatattvasaṃgrahamahāyānābhi-samayamahākalparāja	
	Eng.	The Adamantine Pinnacle Sutra (In Two Esoteric Sutras)	
31–35	*Ch.*	Mo-ho-sêng-ch'i-lü (摩訶僧祇律)	1425
	Skt.	Mahāsāṃghika-vinaya (?)	
36–42	*Ch.*	Ssŭ-fên-lü (四分律)	1428
	Skt.	Dharmaguptaka-vinaya (?)	
43, 44	*Ch.*	Shan-chien-lü-p'i-p'o-sha (善見律毘婆沙)	1462
	Pāli	Samantapāsādikā	
45-I	*Ch.*	Fan-wang-ching (梵網經)	1484
	Skt.	Brahmajāla-sūtra (?)	

Vol. No.		Title	*T.* No.
45-II	*Ch.*	Yu-p'o-sai-chieh-ching (優婆塞戒經)	1488
	Skt.	Upāsakaśīla-sūtra (?)	
	Eng.	The Sutra on Upāsaka Precepts	
46-I	*Ch.*	Miao-fa-lien-hua-ching-yu-po-t'i-shê (妙法蓮華經憂波提舍)	1519
	Skt.	Saddharmapuṇḍarīka-upadeśa	
46-II	*Ch.*	Fo-ti-ching-lun (佛地經論)	1530
	Skt.	Buddhabhūmisūtra-śāstra (?)	
	Eng.	The Interpretation of the Buddha Land	
46-III	*Ch.*	Shê-ta-ch'eng-lun (攝大乘論)	1593
	Skt.	Mahāyānasaṃgraha	
	Eng.	The Summary of the Great Vehicle	
47	*Ch.*	Shih-chu-p'i-p'o-sha-lun (十住毘婆沙論)	1521
	Skt.	Daśabhūmika-vibhāṣā (?)	
48, 49	*Ch.*	A-p'i-ta-mo-chü-shê-lun (阿毘達磨俱舍論)	1558
	Skt.	Abhidharmakośa-bhāṣya	
50–59	*Ch.*	Yü-ch'ieh-shih-ti-lun (瑜伽師地論)	1579
	Skt.	Yogācārabhūmi	
60-I	*Ch.*	Ch'êng-wei-shih-lun (成唯識論)	1585
	Eng.	Demonstration of Consciousness Only (In Three Texts on Consciousness Only)	
60-II	*Ch.*	Wei-shih-san-shih-lun-sung (唯識三十論頌)	1586
	Skt.	Triṃśikā	
	Eng.	The Thirty Verses on Consciousness Only (In Three Texts on Consciousness Only)	
60-III	*Ch.*	Wei-shih-êrh-shih-lun (唯識二十論)	1590
	Skt.	Viṃśatikā	
	Eng.	The Treatise in Twenty Verses on Consciousness Only (In Three Texts on Consciousness Only)	
61-I	*Ch.*	Chung-lun (中論)	1564
	Skt.	Madhyamaka-śāstra	
61-II	*Ch.*	Pien-chung-pien-lun (辯中邊論)	1600
	Skt.	Madhyāntavibhāga	

Vol. No.		Title	T. No.
61-III	*Ch.*	Ta-ch'eng-ch'êng-yeh-lun (大乘成業論)	1609
	Skt.	Karmasiddhiprakaraṇa	
61-IV	*Ch.*	Yin-ming-ju-chêng-li-lun (因明入正理論)	1630
	Skt.	Nyāyapraveśa	
61-V	*Ch.*	Chin-kang-chên-lun (金剛針論)	1642
	Skt.	Vajrasūcī	
61-VI	*Ch.*	Chang-so-chih-lun (彰所知論)	1645
62	*Ch.*	Ta-ch'eng-chuang-yen-ching-lun (大乘莊嚴經論)	1604
	Skt.	Mahāyānasūtrālaṃkāra	
63-I	*Ch.*	Chiu-ching-i-ch'eng-pao-hsing-lun (究竟一乘寶性論)	1611
	Skt.	Ratnagotravibhāgamahāyānottaratantra-śāstra	
63-II	*Ch.*	P'u-t'i-hsing-ching (菩提行經)	1662
	Skt.	Bodhicaryāvatāra	
63-III	*Ch.*	Chin-kang-ting-yü-ch'ieh-chung-fa-a-nou-to-lo-san-miao-san-p'u-t'i-hsin-lun (金剛頂瑜伽中發阿耨多羅三藐三菩提心論)	1665
63-IV	*Ch.*	Ta-ch'eng-ch'i-hsin-lun (大乘起信論)	1666
	Skt.	Mahāyānaśraddhotpāda-śāstra (?)	
63-V	*Ch.*	Na-hsien-pi-ch'iu-ching (那先比丘經)	1670
	Pāli	Milindapañhā	
64	*Ch.*	Ta-ch'eng-chi-p'u-sa-hsüeh-lun (大乘集菩薩學論)	1636
	Skt.	Śikṣāsamuccaya	
65	*Ch.*	Shih-mo-ho-yen-lun (釋摩訶衍論)	1688
66-I	*Ch.*	Pan-jo-po-lo-mi-to-hsin-ching-yu-tsan (般若波羅蜜多心經幽賛)	1710
	Eng.	A Comprehensive Commentary on the Heart Sutra (Prajñāpāramitā-hṛdaya-sūtra)	
66-II	*Ch.*	Kuan-wu-liang-shou-fo-ching-shu (觀無量壽佛經疏)	1753
66-III	*Ch.*	San-lun-hsüan-i (三論玄義)	1852

Vol. No.		Title	*T*. No.
66-IV	*Ch.*	Chao-lun (肇論)	1858
67, 68	*Ch.*	Miao-fa-lien-hua-ching-hsüan-i (妙法蓮華經玄義)	1716
69	*Ch.*	Ta-ch'eng-hsüan-lun (大乘玄論)	1853
70-I	*Ch.*	Hua-yen-i-ch'eng-chiao-i-fên-ch'i-chang (華嚴一乘教義分齊章)	1866
70-II	*Ch.*	Yüan-jên-lun (原人論)	1886
70-III	*Ch.*	Hsiu-hsi-chih-kuan-tso-ch'an-fa-yao (修習止觀坐禪法要)	1915
70-IV	*Ch.*	T'ien-t'ai-ssŭ-chiao-i (天台四教儀)	1931
71, 72	*Ch.*	Mo-ho-chih-kuan (摩訶止觀)	1911
73-I	*Ch.*	Kuo-ch'ing-pai-lu (國清百録)	1934
73-II	*Ch.*	Liu-tsu-ta-shih-fa-pao-t'an-ching (六祖大師法寶壇經)	2008
	Eng.	The Platform Sutra of the Sixth Patriarch	
73-III	*Ch.*	Huang-po-shan-tuan-chi-ch'an-shih-ch'uan-hsin-fa-yao (黄檗山斷際禪師傳心法要)	2012A
73-IV	*Ch.*	Yung-chia-chêng-tao-ko (永嘉證道歌)	2014
74-I	*Ch.*	Chên-chou-lin-chi-hui-chao-ch'an-shih-wu-lu (鎭州臨濟慧照禪師語録)	1985
	Eng.	The Recorded Sayings of Linji (In Three Chan Classics)	
74-II	*Ch.*	Wu-mên-kuan (無門關)	2005
	Eng.	Wumen's Gate (In Three Chan Classics)	
74-III	*Ch.*	Hsin-hsin-ming (信心銘)	2010
	Eng.	The Faith-Mind Maxim (In Three Chan Classics)	
74-IV	*Ch.*	Ch'ih-hsiu-pai-chang-ch'ing-kuei (勅修百丈清規)	2025

Vol. No.		Title	T. No.
75	*Ch.*	Fo-kuo-yüan-wu-ch'an-shih-pi-yen-lu (佛果圜悟禪師碧巖録)	2003
	Eng.	The Blue Cliff Record	
76-I	*Ch.*	I-pu-tsung-lun-lun (異部宗輪論)	2031
	Skt.	Samayabhedoparacanacakra	
76-II	*Ch.*	A-yü-wang-ching (阿育王經)	2043
	Skt.	Aśokarāja-sūtra (?)	
	Eng.	The Biographical Scripture of King Aśoka	
76-III	*Ch.*	Ma-ming-p'u-sa-ch'uan (馬鳴菩薩傳)	2046
	Eng.	The Life of Aśvaghoṣa Bodhisattva (In Lives of Great Monks and Nuns)	
76-IV	*Ch.*	Lung-shu-p'u-sa-ch'uan (龍樹菩薩傳)	2047
	Eng.	The Life of Nāgārjuna Bodhisattva (In Lives of Great Monks and Nuns)	
76-V	*Ch.*	P'o-sou-p'an-tou-fa-shih-ch'uan (婆藪槃豆法師傳)	2049
	Eng.	Biography of Dharma Master Vasubandhu (In Lives of Great Monks and Nuns)	
76-VI	*Ch.*	Pi-ch'iu-ni-ch'uan (比丘尼傳)	2063
	Eng.	Biographies of Buddhist Nuns (In Lives of Great Monks and Nuns)	
76-VII	*Ch.*	Kao-sêng-fa-hsien-ch'uan (高僧法顯傳)	2085
	Eng.	The Journey of the Eminent Monk Faxian (In Lives of Great Monks and Nuns)	
76-VIII	*Ch.*	Yu-fang-chi-ch'ao: T'ang-ta-ho-shang-tung-chêng-ch'uan (遊方記抄: 唐大和上東征傳)	2089-(7)
77	*Ch.*	Ta-t'ang-ta-tz'ŭ-ên-ssŭ-san-ts'ang-fa-shih-ch'uan (大唐大慈恩寺三藏法師傳)	2053
	Eng.	A Biography of the Tripiṭaka Master of the Great Ci'en Monastery of the Great Tang Dynasty	
78	*Ch.*	Kao-sêng-ch'uan (高僧傳)	2059
79	*Ch.*	Ta-t'ang-hsi-yü-chi (大唐西域記)	2087
	Eng.	The Great Tang Dynasty Record of the Western Regions	

Vol. No.		Title	*T.* No.
80	*Ch.*	Hung-ming-chi (弘明集)	2102
81–92	*Ch.*	Fa-yüan-chu-lin (法苑珠林)	2122
93-I	*Ch.*	Nan-hai-chi-kuei-nei-fa-ch'uan (南海寄歸内法傳)	2125
	Eng.	Buddhist Monastic Traditions of Southern Asia	
93-II	*Ch.*	Fan-yü-tsa-ming (梵語雜名)	2135
94-I	*Jp.*	Shō-man-gyō-gi-sho (勝鬘經義疏)	2185
94-II	*Jp.*	Yui-ma-kyō-gi-sho (維摩經義疏)	2186
95	*Jp.*	Hok-ke-gi-sho (法華義疏)	2187
96-I	*Jp.*	Han-nya-shin-gyō-hi-ken (般若心經秘鍵)	2203
96-II	*Jp.*	Dai-jō-hos-sō-ken-jin-shō (大乘法相研神章)	2309
96-III	*Jp.*	Kan-jin-kaku-mu-shō (觀心覺夢鈔)	2312
97-I	*Jp.*	Ris-shū-kō-yō (律宗綱要)	2348
	Eng.	The Essentials of the Vinaya Tradition	
97-II	*Jp.*	Ten-dai-hok-ke-shū-gi-shū (天台法華宗義集)	2366
	Eng.	The Collected Teachings of the Tendai Lotus School	
97-III	*Jp.*	Ken-kai-ron (顯戒論)	2376
97-IV	*Jp.*	San-ge-gaku-shō-shiki (山家學生式)	2377
98-I	*Jp.*	Hi-zō-hō-yaku (秘藏寶鑰)	2426
98-II	*Jp.*	Ben-ken-mitsu-ni-kyō-ron (辨顯密二教論)	2427
98-III	*Jp.*	Soku-shin-jō-butsu-gi (即身成佛義)	2428
98-IV	*Jp.*	Shō-ji-jis-sō-gi (聲字實相義)	2429
98-V	*Jp.*	Un-ji-gi (吽字義)	2430
98-VI	*Jp.*	Go-rin-ku-ji-myō-hi-mitsu-shaku (五輪九字明秘密釋)	2514

Vol. No.		Title	*T.* No.
98-VII	*Jp.*	Mitsu-gon-in-hotsu-ro-san-ge-mon (密嚴院發露懺悔文)	2527
98-VIII	*Jp.*	Kō-zen-go-koku-ron (興禪護國論)	2543
98-IX	*Jp.*	Fu-kan-za-zen-gi (普勧坐禪儀)	2580
99–103	*Jp.*	Shō-bō-gen-zō (正法眼藏)	2582
104-I	*Jp.*	Za-zen-yō-jin-ki (坐禪用心記)	2586
104-II	*Jp.*	Sen-chaku-hon-gan-nen-butsu-shū (選擇本願念佛集)	2608
	Eng.	Senchaku Hongan Nembutsu Shū	
104-III	*Jp.*	Ris-shō-an-koku-ron (立正安國論)	2688
	Eng.	Risshōankokuron or The Treatise on the Establishment of the Orthodox Teaching and the Peace of the Nation (In Two Nichiren Texts)	
104-IV	*Jp.*	Kai-moku-shō (開目抄)	2689
	Eng.	Kaimokushō or Liberation from Blindness	
104-V	*Jp.*	Kan-jin-hon-zon-shō (觀心本尊抄)	2692
	Eng.	Kanjinhonzonsho or The Most Venerable One Revealed by Introspecting Our Minds for the First Time at the Beginning of the Fifth of the Five Five Hundred-year Ages (In Two Nichiren Texts)	
104-VI	*Ch.*	Fu-mu-ên-chung-ching (父母恩重經)	2887
105-I	*Jp.*	Ken-jō-do-shin-jitsu-kyō-gyō-shō-mon-rui (顯淨土眞實教行証文類)	2646
105-II	*Jp.*	Tan-ni-shō (歎異抄)	2661
	Eng.	Tannishō: Passages Deploring Deviations of Faith	
106-I	*Jp.*	Ren-nyo-shō-nin-o-fumi (蓮如上人御文)	2668
	Eng.	Rennyo Shōnin Ofumi: The Letters of Rennyo	
106-II	*Jp.*	Ō-jō-yō-shū (往生要集)	2682
107-I	*Jp.*	Has-shū-kō-yō (八宗綱要)	蔵外
	Eng.	The Essentials of the Eight Traditions	

Vol. No.		Title	*T.* No.
107-II	*Jp.*	San-gō-shī-ki （三教指帰）	蔵外
107-III	*Jp.*	Map-pō-tō-myō-ki （末法燈明記）	蔵外
	Eng.	The Candle of the Latter Dharma	
107-IV	*Jp.*	Jū-shichi-jō-ken-pō （十七條憲法）	蔵外